Testimonials

"Yuval Ron's lucid and engaging book shows how the 'Vibrations of the Ultimate' found in the music of the mystical traditions of the world religions are a vital source for all who are seeking deeper connection with the Divine and with each other on the path to authentic selfhood. Read and treasure this book."

> ~ **Bernard McGinn, Ph.D.,** Professor Emeritus of Historical Theology and History of Christianity at the University of Chicago Divinity School, and author of *Presence of God, The Varieties of Vernacular Mysticism, The Mystical Thought of Meister Eckhart, The Foundations of Mysticism,* and *Mystical Union in Judaism, Christianity, and Islam.*

"In an age when religion has too often become a source of conflict, the great mystical traditions of the world serve as a signpost to a new consciousness pointing us toward unity and ecstasy. *Divine Attunement* celebrates the intoxicated spirit of these mystical traditions through music and movement, poetry and prose. I encourage anyone interested in the transformative power and promise of the mystic to read this book and join Yuval Ron on his inspiring and enchanting spiritual journey."

> ~ **Varun Soni, Ph.D.,** Dean of Religious Life at University of Southern California, advisor to the Hindu American Seva Charities, Interfaith Youth Corps, and Parliament of the World's Religions, and author of *Natural Mystics: The Prophetic Lives of Bob Marley and Nusrat Fateh Ali Khan.*

"In Damanhur, we cherish the power and mystery of music, which is why Yuval's book grabs my soul with such a magnetic force. The 'Music of the Plants' is just one way Damanhur taps the sacred and organic matrix of music, and our rituals are replete with sound that creates access to levels of Divinity. I heartily endorse this book and encourage readers to experiment with Yuval's meditative exercises as a pathway to the sacred."

> ~ **Betsy Pool,** Writer-Producer and Director of Integrated Media Strategy for the Federation of Damanhur in Italy.

"Yuval Ron takes us on an intimate journey into the heart and soul of sacred music. Having surrendered himself as an Instrument of Peace, Yuval shares secrets of the Beloved as only a Lover can do. Through timeless stories, modern science and personal experience, Yuval gently lifts the veils so we can glimpse the Invisible Intelligence that is guiding all the cosmos and calling us home through song and dance. *Divine Attunement* is a gift for any spiritual seeker awakening to the ecstasy of her/his own divinity."

~ **Philip M. Hellmich,** Director of Peace at The Shift Network, advisor to the Global Peace Initiative of Women, co-author of *The Love: Of the Fifth Spiritual Paradigm*, and author of *God and Conflict: A Search for Peace in a Time of Crisis.*

"On countless occasions I have been both witness and party to the enchantment created by Yuval Ron and his interfaith ensemble, in America and abroad. Audiences are time and again mesmerized. How lucky for us that Yuval has taken up his pen – in addition to his oud – to help us understand the historical and mystical antecedents of 'musical entrancement' and its potential to heal a broken world. This book is a gift to music lovers and to all who are eager to learn how music and dance ultimately twine heaven to earth."

~ **Ruth Broyde Sharone,** Interfaith activist, filmmaker, Co-Chair of the Southern California Parliament of the World's Religions, correspondent for *The Interfaith Observer*, and author of the prize-winning interfaith memoir *Minefields & Miracles: Why God and Allah Need to Talk.*

"Music is the language of the soul. In the powerful and poetic reflections of master musician Yuval Ron, we learn that music has the power to connect our souls to one another in a loving circle of dance and prayer and ultimately connect our souls to the Source of All. Drawing from multiple traditions of wisdom and mysticism, Yuval raises our horizons to know the greater unity within the melody of all human experience. *Divine Attunement* is a masterpiece worthy of deep reflection."

~ **Rabbi Edward Feinstein,** Senior Rabbi at Valley Beth Shalom, and author of *Jews and Judaism in the 21st Century, Tough Questions Jews Ask: A Young Adult's Guide to Building a Jewish Life*, and *Capturing the Moon.*

"Yuval Ron's artistic and insightful work is a waft of jasmine from the hem of the Divine Beloved. I have always deeply admired his ecstatic and uplifting music, which seems to descend from some celestial inner-realm. Now we have a gracefully written personal memoir, suffused with lyric tales and interwoven with the latest research on the science of music and altered states. This polished gem is a 'must read' for anyone traveling the mystic path and interested in the power of music to transform and transport us to our heavenly abode."

~ **Andrew Vidich, Ph.D.,** Transformational speaker, leadership consultant, and award-winning author of *Light upon Light: 5 Master Pathways to Awaken the Mindful Self.*

"Yuval perfectly describes the ecstatic union of breath and body. He explains how *nafass* (breath) and somatic synergy open a gateway deep within our being where religion, gender, spirituality, dogma, and 'I' disappear … into sacred silent ecstatic Oneness. As children, we inherently knew to twirl and swirl to the point of pure pleasure every chance we could! Yuval shares his clear knowing and experience with the Divine – an exquisite reading on the wisdom of the ages."

~ **Lisa Sahakian,** Founder of Self Mastery Coaching, owner of Inspired Living, host of INlightenUP Radio, and author of *Seven Steps to Self Mastery, Inspired Living Daily Affirmations*, and the *Self Mastery Series* audio set.

"An incredible book by a master musician and storyteller! Yuval opens a fascinating window into the world of sacred practice by presenting historical and legendary tales from Sufi, Hassidic, Gypsy, Christian, Arabic, Hindu, and Zen traditions – *stories that will bring tears to your eyes*. This unique book shows how music has the power to heal and transform one's life, opening doors to creativity and supporting the spiritual quest – a delight for anyone seeking to explore deeper aspects of a meaningful and purposeful life."

~ **Mark Robert Waldman,** Professor of Business at Loyola Marymount University, author of *Words Can Change Your Brain*, and co-author of *Why We Believe What We Believe, Born to Believe*, and *How God Changes Your Brain: Breakthrough Findings from a Leading Neuroscientist.*

"The self that is open and free is a *listening* self, and music, like compassionate dialogue, can bestow the divine gift of truly listening. Yuval expresses the sacred power of music to awaken this openness, this transformation from the 'I' to the 'we,' the illuminating transformation from a particular self to a universal self. Like the *Earth Constitution,* which creates the framework for universal dialogue, planetary peace, and a culture of love, *Divine Attunement* shows the role of music in building this new world. This is a book that should be read by all those who love music, and by all those who simply want to be true lovers."

> ~ **Glen T. Martin, Ph.D.,** Professor of Philosophy and Religious Studies and Chair of Peace Studies at Radford University, President of the World Constitution and Parliament Association, recipient of the Gusi International Peace Prize, and author of *Anatomy of a Sustainable World, Millennium Dawn: The Philosophy of Planetary Crisis and Human Liberation,* and *The Earth Federation Movement: Founding a Global Social Contract.*

"This is a book in which refined qualities of soul shine forth with rare beauty and simplicity. There is a transparency in this work that reflects Yuval Ron's dedication to the well-being and wholeness of others, as narrated in stories and imaged in a musical context meant to inspire and uplift. There is illumined love at the center, breathed into the stories, animating them with all the joy and hope of human aspiration. Mysticism, science, art, poetry, music and above all, a soul resonant with sacred depths, meld into multiple narrative forms, all vivid with intense spiritual dedication. It is a work to treasure, an author to admire, and a deep pleasure to read."

> ~ **Lee Irwin, Ph.D.,** Professor of Religious Studies at the College of Charleston, Vice President of the Association for the Study of Esotericism, and author of *The Dream Seekers, Awakening to Spirit: On Life, Illumination, and Being, The Alchemy of Soul,* and *Coming Down from Above: Prophecy, Resistance, and Renewal in Native American Religions.*

Divine Attunement:
Music as a Path to Wisdom

Written and Retold by

Yuval Ron

With a Foreword by
Pir Zia Inayat-Khan, Ph.D.

Edited by
Shelley Savren & Laura M. George

Published by The Oracle Institute Press, LLC

A division of The Oracle Institute
A 501(c)(3) educational charity
1990 Battlefield Drive
Independence, Virginia 24348
www.TheOracleInstitute.org

Copyright © 2014 by Yuval Ron

Publisher's Cataloging-in-Publication Data

Ron, Yuval (Composer)
    Divine attunement : music as a path to wisdom /
written and retold by Yuval Ron ; with a foreword by Pir
Zia Inayat-Khan, Ph. D. ; edited by Shelley Savren &
Laura M. George.
    pages cm
    Includes bibliographical references.
    LCCN 2014939142
    ISBN 978-1-937465-16-2 (pbk.)
    ISBN 978-1-937465-17-9 (PDF)
    ISBN 978-1-937465-18-6 (mobi)
    ISBN 978-1-937465-19-3 (epub)
    ISBN 978-1-937465-20-9 (audiobook)

    1. Music--Religious aspects. 2. Music--Health
aspects. 3. Spirituality. 4. Mysticism. I. Title.

ML3921.R66 2014   781.1'2
                QBI14-600086

Book design by Donna Montgomery
Printed and bound in the United States

To my Beloved Children:

Silan & Julien

And to All the Children of the World

Yuval Ron at the conclusion of the "Concert for Unity"

Acknowledgements

Thanks to Linda Cadore, who with great enthusiasm planted the idea of writing this book in my mind; to my trusty editor Shelley Savren, who guided and supported me in transporting the material from transcriptions to actual writings; to Elana Golden, whose wisdom and encouragement have helped this journey to reach this point; to Dr. Debra Jan Bible, for her clever suggestions and corrections; to Linda Cadore, Linda Shivers, Giona Ostinelli, and Neil Bernardo, who transcribed my lectures; to my proof readers Judith Rivin and Jay Johnson, for their kind suggestions; to all the good people of The Oracle Institute and Reverend Laura George, whose contributions to this final product are beyond measure; and especially to my wife Carolyne, for her continuous support and her natural gift to radiate and to see the Light.

Table of Contents

Preface

This book is based on talks, stories, workshops, and interviews presented over the last decade. The stories are based on true historical events and revered legends. The teachings and inspiration these stories carry surpass the significance of any minor details of the narratives. Therefore, I have granted myself the artistic liberty to elaborate and imagine several aspects of these tales with the sole purpose of providing dramatic and engaging contexts for the messages. I am grateful to all the caring and loving people who helped me put this material together into a book. My only aspiration is that this little book may help increase the Light in the lives of as many people as possible.

Proceeds from sales of this book will go to benefit charity organizations which support feeding the hungry, spreading knowledge, and promoting peace. For an updated list of the charitable organizations benefiting from this project, please contact Info@YuvalRonMusic.com.

Yuval Ron

Los Angeles, 2014

Foreword

Once it happened that a certain man, while walking with the Sufi Ibrahim Khawwas,[i] was moved to break into song. He intoned:

> *People well know that I am a lover;*
> *But they know not whom I love.*
> *There is no beauty in the human being,*
> *Lovelier than a beautiful voice.*

Ibrahim asked his companion to sing the couplet again. When he did so, Ibrahim danced in ecstasy. So lithely did he step, he seemed to be treading on soft wax rather than hard stone. Then he collapsed in a swoon. When he awoke, he said, "I was in the Garden of Paradise, but you did not see it."[ii]

The message of this charming story is clear: *Music has the power to unveil the garden of eternal beauty.* Or, at least, the best and truest music has this power, when heard with a keen ear and a heeding heart.

Yuval Ron, whom I am blessed to count as a friend, is a troubadour of the music of the soul. When he and his ensemble play, heaven feels tangibly near.

---

i Shaykh Ibrahim al-Khawwas (*circa* 900 C.E.) was a Sufi Saint, legendary for his long journeys in the desert and for his ecstatic dancing, which he performed spontaneously and which often ended in unconsciousness.

ii From *Kashf al-Mahjub,* by Ali bin Usman Hujwiri (pp. 534-535); Tehran: Amir Kabir (1957).

Just as music can bring peace to a soul, music can bring peace to the world. Peacemaking between the peoples of the world is Yuval Ron's noble mission. Toward this end, he has for years employed the oud, the ney, and the drum. Now, with this book, Yuval has taken up another instrument – the pen.

So let us listen, with a keen ear and a heeding heart, to the music of his written words.

Pir Zia Inayat-Khan, Ph.D.

The Abode of the Message
New Lebanon, New York
www.TheAbode.org

December 17, 2013
Urs Sharif Hazrat Mawlana Rumi[iii]

---

iii December 17, 2013, marks the 740th anniversary of Mevlana Jalaluddin Rumi's death, when the Sufi master's soul finally united with the Beloved. To Rumi's followers, it is known as *Urs Sharif Hazrat Mawlana Rumi* (the "The Noble Wedding Night of His Holiness, our Master Rumi"). Moreover, December 17 marks a glorious and happy worldwide event – the annual pilgrimage to the holy shrine of Rumi located in Konya, Turkey.

Biography

Pir Zia Inayat-Khan, Ph.D., is a scholar and teacher of Sufism in the lineage of his grandfather Hazrat Inayat Khan, who first brought Sufism to North America and Europe, and his father Pir Vilayat Inayat Khan, who founded Sufi Order International.

When Pir Zia was thirteen, his father sent him to Dharamsala, India, to study under the auspices of his friend, His Holiness the Dalai Lama. Pir Zia received his B.A. (Hons) in Persian Literature from the London School of Oriental and African Studies, and his M.A. and Ph.D. in Religion (Islamic Studies) from Duke University.

Since 2004, Pir Zia has served as President of the Sufi Order International, guiding Sufi communities in North America, South America, Europe, the Middle East, Asia, and the South Pacific. To provide opportunities for intensive Sufi study, Pir Zia founded the Suluk Academy, which offers courses for Sufi initiates in New York, California, and France.

Pir Zia also is the founder of the inter-spiritual institute Seven Pillars House of Wisdom, a Fellow of the Lindisfarne Association, and an Advisor to the Contemplative Alliance. He is the author of *Saracen Chivalry: Counsels on Valor, Generosity, and the Mystical Quest,* and he is the editor of *A Pearl in Wine* and *Caravan of Souls.*

Note from the Publisher

As the worldwide spiritual leader of Sufi Order International, Pir Zia Inayat-Khan purposely chose an auspicious date to compose this Foreword: *Urs Sharif Hazrat Mawlana Rumi,* which is the Holy Anniversary of Rumi's physical departure from the earth plane on December 17, 1273. We are grateful and exceedingly humbled by the honor and blessing which Pir Zia has bestowed upon this interfaith peace project, and we attribute such amazing grace, ultimately, to the Divine.

Don't open the door to the study and begin reading.
Take down a musical instrument.
Let the beauty we love be what we do.

~ Mevlana Jalaluddin Rumi

CHAPTER I

The Golden Thread

Once there was a flautist who fell in love with a mysterious beloved. Without much delay or hesitation, the lover traveled to the house of the beloved and knocked on the door.

"Who is knocking?" asked a quizzing, ancient voice.

"It is I," announced the lover in a breathy and intoned voice. The door remained closed.

The lover sadly went back to his world and his work. He picked up his reed flute and played the most passionate, longing melodies, expressing his love to the enigmatic beloved. Over time, the lover shared his beautiful soulful tunes, and many people came to admire and applaud his fine music.

The lover was proud and pleased indeed. He now felt ready to attempt another visit with his beloved. So he traveled again to the house and knocked on the door.

"Who is knocking?" asked a playful, deep-rooted voice.

"It is I," responded the lover with a trembling voice, yet with a deep sense of worth, power, and true love. Nevertheless, the door remained closed.

The lover, again, went back to his world and his work. Out of despair and confusion, he began playing his flute with no energy at all. It was as though another being were blowing through his flute. At first, only a faint sound came through the reed pipe ... but then it grew and gained strength, until the tone of the flute was unlike any sound he had ever heard. Indeed, the resonance was so pure, so transparent and so exquisite, it seemed as though a golden thread had descended from above, passed through him into the flute and then outward. It was the most exhilarating and inspiring music imaginable.

The wholesomeness of the sound that resonated from his reed and the blissful way that it made him feel aroused the lover to undertake previously unthinkable deeds: *Without any apparent reason, he began helping people – many people – whom he did not even know.*

It was then that the lover completely forgot about himself. Instead, all that concerned him was how to make every living being that crossed his path more joyful. He suddenly realized that throughout his entire life he had focused on bringing happiness to just one person – himself. Now, as he worked to make many *other* people joyful, he actually was spreading much more happiness in the world.

The lover then began to help in anonymous ways, without asking for credit, without mentioning his name. It felt as though it was not even he who was producing all this good will. The amazing golden thread was growing and moving through him, a gift of pure pleasure and ease.

Nearly a year had passed since the lover last visited the house of the beloved, and it occurred to him that it was time to pay another visit. He journeyed to the house, and with a hand motion as light as a feather, the lover knocked on the familiar door.

"Who is knocking?" asked a spirited, primordial voice.

"It is YOU," whispered the lover with a tender, yet knowledgeable voice. Then he pointed toward the locked door and leaned forward. The door swung open ...

This story came to me as a blessing in the midst of a curse. A severe internal infection had kept me in bed for days. The blazing heat and the pulsating headache kept me awake for several nights in a row. The furious fever and the constant pain refused to yield to the various medications the doctors had prescribed. There was no remedy left for me to take or even try, except to search for some blessing in the midst of this torture ...

Finally, during the third sleepless night, my mind began weaving a mystical tale.[1] It was a gift from above – a magical, musical parable. The story unfolded in circular lines that repeated themselves over and over again throughout the night, manifesting a round web of words and images, ever changing in subtle variations until early morning, when the narrative ultimately became clear.

This tale that nursed me through a dark night also worked its way into my ensemble's concert programs to become a source of inspiration to others. I am fond of telling it to the audience just before the whirling dervish joins us on stage for the sacred Sufi music and movement ritual. With the impression of the story still resonating in our hearts, we commence a journey toward the house of the Great Spirit, the Beloved, the One who is the Source of all Life.

---

1 The theme of "knocking on the door of the Beloved" was borrowed from a parable told by the great Sufi mystic Jalaluddin Rumi and recorded in his masterpiece, *The Mathnavi* (*circa* 1270). However, Rumi was not necessarily the first to tell this tale, as this classic theme has been presented in even more ancient works.

CHAPTER II

Sacred Ecstacy

I could hear the seagulls' calls and smell the salty air of the Sea of Marmara from the small café by the grand Blue Mosque of Istanbul. An old man pushed a cart loaded with freshly baked round bread covered with sesame seeds. I felt at home. It was a beautiful warm day in early June 2011, and I was getting ready to start a Peace Mission tour of Turkey. It was a time when I would read one Rumi poem a day and seek wisdom from the great Sufi mystic's timeless teachings.[2]

"More chai?" The waiter brought me some more Turkish tea in a small transparent blue glass shaped in a feminine curve. Sweet tea. Life is good!

---

2 Jalaluddin Muhammad Rumi (1207-1273) was a poet and teacher of the Sufi path, a mystical branch of Islam. His poems have been translated into nearly every language, and many later artists (authors, poets, playwrights, musicians, and dancers) have been divinely inspired by his work. The general themes of Rumi's poetry include the concepts of Oneness and Unity with the Divine, which the seeker has lost and longs to restore.

I opened my book to a random page and received a gift. I was about to spend two weeks with the Sufis and Roma gypsies of Turkey, and Jalaluddin Rumi's poetry provided me with a much-needed perspective. Eight hundred years ago, he observed that artists – unlike seekers who enter the fire of ecstasy – merely flirt with the Divine, flirt with the Creator, the Source of life.

I often have felt transitory connections to a mysterious energy, during graceful and blessed moments that highlight my concerts and workshops. We, the artists, touch this great mystery momentarily ... and then it is lost. The bliss is there one moment and gone the next. Here it is, and there it disappears. Are we flirting with Source, or is it teasing us?

When the Yuval Ron Ensemble supports dervishes with devotional music, as when we participate in the hidden rituals of our Turkish Sufi friends, we provide a runway from which they may fly higher and reach an ecstatic state, the true fire. The sacred ecstasy they experience is above and beyond the mere "flirtation of artists."

This quest for ecstasy has fascinated the Sufis of Islam, the mystics of Judaism (Kabbalistic and Hassidic), as well as the ancient Greeks. Often, ecstasy is connected to music and dance. This brings to mind a tribal circle.

You are there, standing among several indigenous men and women whom you have never met. Everyone around you is drumming and chanting. The drumbeat is tantalizing; it feels so good to be a part of such a group. The collective group's presence slowly overwhelms your individuality. As the beat gets faster and faster, you and everyone around you stop thinking, stop being aware of time, stop being aware of who – you think – you are. And the rhythms and vocal chants drive everybody into an ecstatic trance where there is no self-consciousness or judgment.

Then gradually, the music slows down and fades. You are physically and emotionally exhausted, yet your senses are so sharp, you feel more alive and awake than ever before! You look around, and in a magical way, all your fellow drummers seem simply beautiful. There is a certain smile in their eyes and a misty light over their faces. You feel an intimacy and closeness to them, something you never could have imagined feeling just an hour ago, before the ecstatic drumming began.

This is just one expression of sacred ecstasy, the kind that has been practiced for centuries in tribal societies. It is also an important part of Sufism, Hassidic Judaism and the mystical practices of East Asian religions. The terminology may vary, but the essence is the same: It is an attempt to transcend individual perception, the sense of separation between us and our fellow man and between us and the Creator, and the illusion that the physical world around us is all that exists.[3]

And this illusion is not child's play. It is one of the most powerful misperceptions that we carry with us. Our ordinary five senses inform us that we only exist in the zone between our minds and the tip of our toes, between our brain and our skin. That is the "I" – the individual. The rest of life – including other people, life forms, and the whole universe – we perceive as "they" or the "other" or definitely not "me." Therefore, we un-consciously (and sometimes consciously) focus on the survival of "me" and care much less about how "they" are surviving.

---

3 This illusion (or the veil) of the physical world has been called *maya* by the ancient Hindu religion. There are numerous references to it in various other mystical traditions, such as Kabbalah, Sufism, and Gnostic Christianity.

It appears selfish, but in truth, such a perception is based in fear. In other words, concerns for the survival of "me" are rooted in fear of death and suffering.

Sacred ecstasy takes us beyond this limited view of life. But the journey toward ecstasy is difficult because of the way we are wired. The nature of our mind, our consciousness and possibly even our physicality belie our connection to the All.[4] Is it possible to go beyond ordinary perception?

From ancient time onward, the motivation for attempting this seemingly impossible quest was always connected to the human desire to utilize and to benefit from a superior creative force. For example, a connection to the Divine was deemed necessary for success in shamanic medicine, music, dance, and other spiritual rituals. If a person could connect with or channel super beings or spirits, he or she could become a powerful healer, magician, dancer, musician, or tribal leader. But beyond these practical needs, spiritual experimentation historically has addressed the human *longing* to comprehend and connect to the mystery of all mysteries: the Creator, the Source of all life. Thus, the mystics of all traditions have advised that if we go beyond the mere physical, we may unite with the metaphysical, intangible, spiritual aspect of life.

Every once in a while, I get a call from a university where I am about to give a lecture on "Sacred Ecstasy." The voice on the other end of the line asks, "Would you mind not mentioning the word 'ecstasy' during your visit?"

"Not to worry," I reply. "I won't promote the mind-altering drug that has adopted and misused the word 'ecstasy.'"

All joking aside, I am aware that some young people believe they have experienced "ecstasy" after taking a drug, a chemical

---

4 See the research and theories of neuroscientist Vilayanur Ramachandran, Ph.D., involving phantom limb sensations and the brain. Some of Dr. Ramachandran's studies suggest that physical body parts seem to block brain identification with other human beings outside of us.

short-cut to reaching an altered state of mind. However, let us look up the original meaning of the word.

From the Greek, ecstasy means "to be outside of oneself." In other words, ecstasy permits us to transcend individualistic perception, to sense beyond the regular senses which normally lead us to believe that we do not exist beyond our own flesh and mind. When we truly reach an ecstatic state, we are able to *feel* that we actually exist beyond ourselves. That we *are* everything!

In a sacred, ecstatic state of mind, we feel connected to all living things. We feel that we are within all of creation, and that all of creation is within us. Some might cry out at such a moment, "God is in me!" as some Sufi saints have expressed. But the words are not important; we may call Source anything we like. A deep sense of the unity of all things is what we are seeking – not an intellectual understanding of the idea of unity. It is a gut feeling, a sensation, a perception. Yet, is this a true perception or just another illusion?

The mystics of old have been saying for centuries and in various terms that the unity of all things is the *true* reality. They have insisted that we *do* exist beyond our bodies. Isn't it fascinating that recent research is now confirming that our brain neurons actually reach beyond our bodies, connect with, convey information to, and affect living things *outside* of our bodies![5]

The implications of such neurological studies are far reaching and support the mystic's assertion that we are inseparable from all creation. If we truly feel that we and the "other" are one, if we truly love the "other" as we love ourselves, then peace would be the natural consequence. Having gained this comprehension,

---

5 See various scientific studies of "mirror neurons" – brain cells that interact outside of our bodies and connect us to others beyond our skin. See also an article entitled "Mirror Neurons and Imitation Learning as the Driving Force Behind 'The Great Leap Forward' in Human Evolution," by Dr. Ramachandran (2000) (www. Edge.org/conversation/mirror-neurons-and-imitation-learning-as-the-driving-force-behind-the-great-leap-forward-in-human-evolution).

we would never dump toxic waste in our neighbor's yard, we would be generous with a stranger, and we would never unleash violence in a distant part of the world. That is the essence of the ancient Great Commandment: *Love your neighbor as you love yourself.*[6]

Even though the concept that "you are everything" is extremely difficult for many of us to truly internalize, there are numerous ways to experience it. Within ancient shamanic wisdom, it is told that music and ecstatic movement *can* move us outside of ourselves so that we may reach an altered state of mind – a state of sacred ecstasy – the same goal of ecstatic rituals and celebrations conducted by Hassidic Jews, Sufi Muslims, and Pentecostal Christians. Therefore, the question arises: *Which music and what kind of movement should be used for such an ecstatic journey?*

The Yuval Ron Ensemble with a Sufi Whirling Dervish

---

6 The "Golden Rule" expressed in all religious and indigenous traditions.

It is interesting that both Sufis and Hassidic Jews use circling movements to commence the journey toward sacred ecstasy. The Sufi whirling dervishes take the path of turning around the heart, a practice credited to Rumi, the 13th Century Sufi master. This practice, however, is more ancient than Rumi, as it has been a native practice of the people of Central Asia and the Middle East.[7]

Circling is mentioned in the Hebrew Bible as a form of worship and ritual practiced at the first Jerusalem Temple built by King Solomon. Indeed, the Hebrew word for "holiday" – *chag* – means, literally, to "turn in a circle." And earlier portions of the Bible note that circling is a way to invoke powerful metaphysical powers, as with the circling of Joshua around Jericho. Sacred circling also is a movement used in ecstatic dances at Hassidic wedding parties and by bridegrooms during Jewish Kabbalistic wedding ceremonies. Similarly, in the Islamic tradition, circling is part of the pilgrimage to the holy city of Mecca – a tradition that dates back to the 7th Century, six hundred years before Rumi. Circling the Kaaba, which contains the holy "Black Stone" of Mecca, likely has its roots in pre-Islamic pagan Arabia. This tradition is one of the most ecstatic and hypnotizing rituals in human history.[8]

The Sufis, as with all mystics, prefer the deep poetic meaning over the literal one. And so they ask: *Why go to Mecca, as the real Kaaba is in you? It is in your heart. Circle your heart. That is the sacred stone on which you should focus your attention. That is where you may find the Beloved (the Creator).*

---

7 For example, the Tatar people in Central Asia and the ancient Hebrews and Arabs in the Middle East.

8 This is seen, for example, in the movie "Samsara" by Ron Fricke and Mark Magidson (www.barakasamsara.com). The soundtrack for the film also includes the song "La Illah aillah la/Nigun le Mashiakh" from Yuval Ron's CD *Oud Prayers on the Road to St. Jacques* (www.cdbaby.com/cd/yuval8).

They therefore turn and circle around the inner beauty, the inner "honey," around the divine spark of Light (Kabbalistic terminology)[9] or the *Atman* (in Hinduism). They circle around their own hearts on the way to sacred ecstasy ... just as atoms circle within all particles of nature, as the Earth spins on its own axis while at the same time circling the Sun, all of which are twirling in our galaxy in an ever-expanding universe.[10]

The secret of the circle is its expression of *hypnotic repetition.* And repetition is crucial for the initial stages of the ecstatic mind-altering process, as we will soon see in the case of ecstatic music as well.

The mental journey toward bliss must begin with a gradual surrender of the "watch dog" function of the mind. If you want to lower a person's guard or passively put their mind to rest so that they are less apt to intellectualize, you only need subject them to some type of repeated experience.

Let's say you repeat and repeat and repeat the same pattern in front of a person. It could be the same movement, the same sound, or the same word (if it is a word, it should be repeated with the exact same intonation). Or you may use a visual pattern, by showing a person the same image again and again and again. Better yet, combine *all* the above modalities, and loop them for a good while. The result of this repeated experience is that the person will be subconsciously directed toward an altered state of mind.

---

9 See the DVD *Seeker of Truth* with Dervish Aziz and the Yuval Ron Ensemble at the World Festival of Sacred Music in Los Angeles, CA (2008) (on YouTube: www.youtube.com/watch?v=yJBqAZYIfek; and on Vimeo: www.vimeo.com/2413880).

10 At the equator, the Earth is spinning at over 1,000 mph. The Earth circles the Sun at more than 67,000 mph. And the Milky Way Galaxy is turning at approximately 537,000 mph.

How does it work? First, the lack of new stimuli calms the mind, which then ceases analyzing the sound, movement, or image stimuli. In other words, looping the stimulus tricks the mind into a state of rest. At this point the "guard" is taking a break (a/k/a the "monkey" is sleeping).[11] Now, the mind is primed to advance toward an altered state, ready to receive a new perception of reality.

Yuval Ron leading the audience toward altered states of mind

Music and audio stimulation provides another great method for relaxing, hypnotizing, and altering moods and mental perceptions. That is why the devotional music of the Sufi and Hassidic traditions includes constant repetition of the same melody. What changes is the rate of the musical pulse or beat. People, especially kids, get excited when music and dance are slowly accelerated. The intensifying rhythms help us forget about our inhibitions and promote release of the intellect.

---

11 For a discussion of the "Monkey Mind," see Chapter IV, "Meditation, Unity, and Why Should You Tame the Monkey."

I recall times when my children were small and their young friends would visit. Often, I would play for them the "Bird's Song," an Armenian mountain shepherd melody.[12] As I began to speed up the tempo, the excitement and the joy in the room would build. The children would then run around, waving their little arms like bird wings, racing faster and faster around our living room. The more rapidly I played the music, the more joyful their expressions and the less their self-awareness.

Psycho-acoustic research and clinical studies on music therapy clearly demonstrate that speeding up the pulse of background music drives the listener's heart rate higher.[13] Such accelerated pumping, especially if accompanied by repeated movements such as jumping or turning, leads us to a different state of mind. Thus, musical acceleration, which causes the intensifying of biophysical pulsations in the body, assists us in releasing control of the conscious/intellectual mind. Instinct/ intuition then take over, allowing the mind to focus on more visceral information coming in via the senses of hearing, smelling, and touching. Then, our consciousness may tune to the metaphysical sense of Oneness of all things.

With music, the journey to an ecstatic experience typically starts with a dark, intimate, and introspective tone. Both the Sufi and the Hassid begin with a slow and pleading musical melody, almost a lament, but it is actually the sensation of *longing* that the music evokes. The foundation for this quest is the human condition of separation. The soul is captured in a physical body in a physical world, yearning for Spirit, pleading for Union, aching to reach the Source of life – the powerful energy that is

---

12　The song "Tseter" ("Birds") appears on the Yuval Ron Ensemble CD *Tree of Life* (www.cdbaby.com/cd/yuval5).

13　See the M. H. Thaut article entitled "Physiological and Motor Responses to Music Stimuli," in *Music Therapy in the Treatment of Adults with Mental Disorders: Theoretical Bases and Clinical Interventions*; R. F. Unkefer, Editor; New York: Schirmer (2005).

behind everything. The musical modes (i.e., the musical note combinations) that are used in the Turkish Sufi and Hassidic Jewish traditions share some striking similarities. Both paths employ modes that express pain and longing but – when sped up – evolve into powerful and joyful musical expressions.[14]

The lyrics of the Sufi devotional songs, the *Illahis*, often use poetry from the "School of Love," the work of such masters as Rumi, Yunus and Hafiz, who favor the imagery of lovers – an intimate relationship between the seeker and the Divine. In these poems and songs, the seeker is the lover and the Beloved is the awesome life force behind the reality we see with our eyes. Just like the Sufis, the Hassidic lyrics often express the longing to unite with the Creator. One such song repeats the mantra *Tzama lecha Nafshi*, which means in Hebrew, "My soul is thirsty for you." In the biblical "Song of Songs" (traditionally credited to King Solomon) and in some mystical Kabbalistic poetry, we find the same metaphor of the lovers, which the Sufi poets often used to describe the ecstatic path to Unity.[15]

If a Hassidic song includes lyrics, the words simply become a meditative mantra and fade to the background of the mind, which soon may become ecstatic. Yet, the Hassidic spiritual leaders also have established a tradition of using meaningless syllables, almost gibberish, such as: *lai, lai, lai, bim, bim-bam, zum, zum, zum, ya, ya, ya.*[16] This tradition is called *Nigunim* ("tunes" in Hebrew). These lyric-less tunes provide another way to vocally side-step the intellect. When you utter no words

---

14 Both traditions use the *Hijaz* mode. Listen to the track "Sufi" from the CD *Seeker of Truth* (www.cdbaby.com/cd/yuval9) and "La Illah aillah La/Nigun Le Mashiakh" from the CD *Oud Prayers on the Road to St. Jacques* (www.cdbaby.com/cd/yuval8).

15 See Yehuda Halevi's poem "Yonat Rekhokim."

16 For more on the Hassidic spiritual tradition see Chapter VI, "Master of the Good Name," which tells the story of the Baal Shem Tov, founder of the Hassidic movement.

and all you sing are simple syllables, the mind has nothing to chew on, no food for thought, nothing to analyze and no stimuli for the language center in the brain. Hence, a new portal opens which allows us to enter into an ecstatic mind-set.

Kabbalistic terminology which is used by the Jewish mystics to describe the process of sacred ecstasy gives us further hints about what is occurring. That embrace of lovers which the Sufis seek is called *Dvekut* by the mystic Kabbalists. This is a difficult word to translate in English. It comes from the root of the Hebrew word *devek*, which means "glue." In our context, it means "adhesive" or "to bond," which implies strong connections, like friendship, marriage, and ultimately Union – all of which are a part of love. This incredibly emotional process of bonding with the Divine – reaching out and attaching one's soul to the Source of life, getting glued to it, and potentially achieving Union – is perfectly encompassed in the loaded Hebrew word *Dvekut*.

One may be led toward such a mystical bond through Hassidic music and movement, but there is another aspect to consider. The Kabbalistic word *hitlahavut* provides yet another clue on how to attain sacred ecstasy. *Hitlahavut* means "excitement," but upon closer examination, we find that it contains the shorter Hebrew word *lahav*, which means both "blade" and "flame." Thus, as the music gets faster and the circular repeated movements hypnotize and disengage the analytical mind, the seeker becomes excited (the state of *hitlahavut*). The seeker then goes "into the flame" or "becomes the flame." The ecstatic fire acts as a sharp blade (*lahav*) which cuts through the illusion of the physical world to access higher realms. Then the soul (*neshama*) may reach the spiritual dimension for the sake of Union (*Dvekut*).

Whether it is an embrace of lovers or a fiery bonding of the soul, the Sufi and Hassidic paths to Union are paved with soulful music, circular movements, and gradual acceleration of the musical pace and the pulse of the human heart. The fire ...

the blade … the drum … the soulful cry of the reed flute or the singer – all tell the intellect to take a break so that the mind may stop analyzing and allow the soul to fly as high as a dove and to circle, whirl, and twist itself about the Beloved.

At the small café in Istanbul, I drank another cup of sweet chai tea, as the narrow streets became noisy and crowded with people on their way to work. From my vantage point, I saw seagulls flying in circles over the Blue Mosque and down toward the salty Sea of Marmara. Were they merely looking for food? Or was it possible that the birds, like our souls, also were in search of spiritual nourishment? Perhaps they were searching for such emotional sustenance while spinning on high, flirting with bliss, and circling the Mystery of all mysteries.

CHAPTER III

Far Away Dove

It was a hot day in mid-August in the year 1492. The Sultan was sitting on his throne in the grand palace of the illustrious city of Istanbul. Through the large widows he could see the blue water of the Sea of Marmara shining in the sun and the large boats of commerce floating back and forth.

The Sultan was sleepy after a long night of music, women and Turkish delights, when his chief advisor rushed into the royal chamber. "Our magnificent Sultan, have you heard the news? The Queen of Spain has just announced that all the Spanish citizens of Jewish heritage must leave the kingdom! And not only the unemployed are to be banished – the financial advisors to the Royal Spanish court, the top doctors, philosophers, scientists, musicians, poets, print makers, astronomers, translators and educators must all depart at once!"

The Sultan scratched his head, his mind struggling with this confusing news. It sounded like a riddle. "Has the Queen of Spain lost her mind?" he wondered. "Why would she do this to her own great empire, a kingdom that just recently gathered the tools and means to send explorers to search for new worlds? And much of the fortune and capabilities for such a grand mission are available thanks to these people she is now ordering away!"

As these and many other confusing thoughts were circling around his feverish mind, the Sultan suddenly arrived at a brilliant idea. "Admiral Reis!" roared the Sultan at the commander of the Ottoman navy. "At once, direct our fearsome fleet to the shores of Al Andalus in the Spanish Kingdom. Announce to all the Jewish refugees that the Sultan himself has granted a free ride and safe passage on the great Ottoman navy ships and boats. And it is indeed a complimentary service, granted that the *only* and *final* destination is Turkey!"

And so in the summer of 1492, over a hundred thousand Jews boarded Ottoman ships and were given a new prosperous life within the Ottoman Empire.[17]

One of the people on these boats was a young rabbi carrying a small leather bag. It was the only thing he could take with him; everything else had to be left behind. He and all the other outcasts lost their homes, estates, jobs and everything that had been earned while the Jews were Spanish citizens for six hundred years. The young rabbi knew that inside the leather bag there was something his family had treasured and kept for at least four hundred years. He had no idea what it was, but certainly he knew he must not depart without it. His duty was to guard it well on this new faithful journey, out of one diaspora and into the next.

After the young Spanish rabbi settled into a new home in the Ottoman lands, he found a well-paid position and even

---

17 A Muslim-Turkish empire formed in 1299 that reigned over the Middle East, southeastern Europe, northern Africa, and western Asia for over 600 years. The Ottoman Empire welcomed Jews who were banished by the Christian nations. The empire was dissolved after World War I and separated into numerous nations.

managed to form new friendships with some local dervishes. Only then did he finally take a moment to sit down and open the leather bag. Inside, there were papers. Just papers. "What kind of treasure is this?" he wondered.

Almost immediately, it became clear to him that the manuscript was written in the sacred language his people used only for prayer in the synagogues. Yet, he noticed that it was not one of the sacred texts of the Hebrew Bible. Rather, it was an old manuscript probably from the 11th Century written in Andalusia by the great Hebrew mystic poet and philosopher Rabbi Yehuda Halevi. The treasure his ancestors kept for four hundred years was an original manuscript of Hebrew poems.

The young rabbi pulled one loose paper from the pack and read it aloud. It was a poem about a dove, a bird from far away, flying into the forest. But the bird was wounded and had fallen to the ground. She was unable to fly anymore. Then all of a sudden, the dove began to move! She turned and turned around herself, whirling around in circles. And then she began to fly in spirals, in an emotional storm. Lifted by the wind, she spun and soared up above!

"But how could a wounded bird take flight and soar again? How could it be?" the rabbi pondered. The answer was revealed in the following poetic line: *The dove had seen her Beloved, and this precious sight carried her up high to circle about him in a tempest of passion and exhilaration.*[18]

It was a beautiful and most enchanting poem and it touched the young rabbi deeply. He realized that the dove was not just a dove; she was a symbol for something else. He knew the dove stood for the soul and the Beloved for the Master of the Universe, the Source of Life.[19] But what he could not comprehend was

---

18 In the original Hebrew text it is the word *Doda* (her lover) – a code word in mystical Sufi and Hebrew poetry for the Divine.

19 The common interpretation of the dove image within the Jewish tradition is a symbol for the nation of Israel (Knesset Israel).

how those images of her turning and whirling on the way to the Beloved – the exact images and movements used by his new Sufi friends, the dervishes of Turkey – also were recorded in a Hebrew poem from 11th Century Spain, four hundred years earlier!

These enigmatic Muslim dervishes, whom he now befriended, also spun and turned and whirled around in a ritual of remembrance and invocation of the Source of Life. These followers of Rumi, the great Sufi sage of the 13th Century, used the same terminology of Love, the same kind of poetry! But how did Rabbi Yehuda Halevy know all this back in Spain hundreds of years before Rumi?

This question haunted his mind, day and night, night and day, and would not dissipate. The young rabbi felt there was something he was not grasping, something far more complicated and mysterious than anything he was exposed to during all his rabbinical studies. So he made up his mind to go to Baghdad, because in that ancient city lived a very old rabbi everyone called the "Mastermind." Indeed, it was said that the old master had the answer to any question, no matter how mysterious!

Soon thereafter, the young rabbi began his pilgrimage, traveling by foot all the way to Baghdad. He carried with him the precious manuscript, which he finally presented to the old master. He then asked the old man the question that had been haunting him, and he waited silently and patiently to hear the answer.

"Oh, it is very simple, very simple indeed," said the Mastermind in a piercing raspy voice. "It all has to do with Andalusia, where the great scholars and mystic poets of Judaism and Islam mingled for many years and enriched each other's teachings and poetry. And in the days of Rabbi Yehuda Halevy, there was a noble Andalusian Sufi sheikh called Ibn Arabi, who was also a great philosopher and mystic poet. Ibn Arabi traveled all the way to Damascus where he met Rumi … and that is the connection. That is the answer to your question, my boy."

"But you know," he added suddenly, almost in a secretive whisper, "this knowledge, this hidden wisdom is actually *much* older than Spain. It is an old teaching from the Middle East, from our ancient ancestors.[20] It is a *secret* wisdom we all share – we the sons of Abraham who were open to receive it, we the people of the desert, both Muslims and Jews."

The young rabbi was profoundly moved to hear that his people, the Hebrews, and his new friends in Turkey, the Sufi dervishes, followers of the Prophet,[21] both shared the same secret wisdom, which originated from the birthplace of their faiths and teachings. Tears of gratitude appeared in the corners of his eyes. He was so deeply inspired by this new insight that a new melody sprang out of his heart, a tune that perfectly fit the Hebrew words of the old manuscript, the words of the poem about the far away dove. And spontaneously, right there in front of the old master, he sang the new song, which he composed on the spot. It was a unique and soulful tune about the injured dove, how she miraculously flew in circles and how she turned and whirled around the Beloved. Anyone listening could envision the desperate flight, the feel and longing in the music!

However, the Mastermind of Baghdad motioned with disapproval. "I do *not* like this song, because you have used a musical modality that we Iraqis – both Jews and Muslims – do not favor and very seldom use!"

The young rabbi was completely crushed. He felt tears choking him deep inside his throat. What could he say to this old master, the genius of a generation, the one rabbi who knew the answers to all of life's questions?

After a short while, the young Spanish rabbi just stood up, turned around, and went out the door saying nothing. He was stunned, as if someone had hit him on the head with a big wooden log.

---

20 See the mystical love poem *Song of Songs* from the Hebrew Bible, written according to Jewish tradition by King Solomon in Jerusalem around 950 B.C.E.

21 Prophet Muhammad, founder of the Islamic path.

Yet, as he slowly walked down the street, he simply could not contain himself, and he began to hum the new tune. He sang the song he had fashioned from the poem, first quietly to himself. Then he sang it louder – again and again and again – with almost uncontrollable obsession:

Hitofefa, hitnofefa, chofefa;
Saviv le Doda, sochara, soara.

She flew away, blown away;
Circling in precise orbits around her Beloved;
She turned and whirled, in an emotional, passionate storm.

At that very moment, on that very street, a family gathered on their balcony and heard the song. And they liked it! They were not *supposed* to like it, because they were an Iraqi family, a Jewish Iraqi family that normally would not use such a musical mode. Nevertheless, they took it to heart and taught the song to their children, and to their children's children, a practice they continued for many, many years …

And thus it came to pass that one family – just one family – kept the song about the far away dove alive, handing it down from one generation to the next and preserving it for five centuries.[22]

---

22 I am grateful to the Ovadya Ftaya family who preserved the song about the dove, and to my dear friend Rabbi Haim Ovadia who shared the precious memory of his grandfather singing it and invoking the presence of the dove in little Haim's mind and heart. Rabbi Haim never would have shared the history of the song with me, except for the fact that an Israeli musicologist who specialized in the Iraqi-Jewish tradition concluded that the song was composed in *makam Nahawand* – a rare musical mode within the Iraqi tradition – and that only one family, the Ovadya Ftaya, knew this song.

Today along the small stone-paved streets of the old city of Jerusalem, you may hear the soft voice of a man singing that very song, as he slowly walks to synagogue in the early morning hour, singing about the dove and reaching toward the heavens.[23] And in the old city of Konya, the dervishes of Mevlana still turn and whirl in old rooms covered with Turkish rugs. Their souls yearn for and circle around the same Beloved … the same Infinite Light.

This story formed in my mind one morning when I was preparing a concert program in Berkeley, California. While it is based on historical research of the 1492 Spanish expulsion, the Ottoman Empire, the relations of Jewish Kabbalists and Sufi mystics, and the connection of Ibn Arabi and Rumi, the characters and the meeting of the young rabbi and the "Mastermind of Baghdad" are the fruit of an inspired mind.

---

23 You may hear cantor Yehuda Ovadya Ftaya and Ha'Yonah Ensemble sing the song "Yonat Rechokim" ("A Far Away Dove") on the CD *Yonat Rechokim*. You also may hear Yuval Ron's oud solo version of the song on his CD entitled *Oud Prayers on the Road to St. Jacques*, Track 1, "Yonat Rekhokim" ("Dove of Far Away") (www.cdbaby.com/cd/yuval8).

CHAPTER IV

Meditation, Unity, and Why You Should Tame the Monkey

When I look at you,
I see separation.
Yet when I see you,
I know I am you.

Which one is the illusion? The mystics had no doubt. They found the answer in introspective study of their inner reality and in sacred ecstatic practices. Nowadays in medical centers around the world, neuroscientists are conducting studies that indicate the mystics were on the right track.[24]

Hazrat Inayat Khan, the master musician who brought the Indian version of Sufism to the West, once observed that the scientist and the yogi do similar work. Both examine the universe

---

24 See research described in *How God Changes Your Brain*, by Andrew Newberg, M.D., and Mark Robert Waldman (2010).

by performing various experiments. The difference is that the scientist observes the cosmos from the outside, while the yogi studies the cosmos from within.

Some of the earliest yogic investigations resulted in the knowledge contained in the ancient Vedic texts and wisdom traditions of India. How did these ancient yogis research the mystery of all mysteries without the tools of modern science? By sitting. Simply sitting. And sitting silently. They then developed a repertoire of introspective practices which stilled their minds and allowed them to achieve alternative states of consciousness in which advanced observations and explorations took place.

We are all familiar with three states of consciousness: sleeping, dreaming, and being awake. But could there be more states of consciousness? Are there other ways to experience life?

In the 1980s, researchers at UCLA categorized a fourth state of consciousness.[25] In this state, the body is relaxed and the mind is free to act as a "witness" of its own internal process, like a mirror. While in this state, we feel no emotions, no attachments, just a steady reflection of what is. And in the reflection of this clean and true mirror, we may finally arrive at a grand view of the universal drama. Regardless of where you are looking, and no matter which act of that drama called "life" you are witnessing, the grand view always reveals the same image: *the unity of all things.*

I remember exploring this challenging practice during my days in Berklee College of Music in Boston. Although I was focused on learning the art of composing music for film, the professor who fascinated me the most wasn't one of my music

---

25 The existence of a fourth state of consciousness was proposed in the early 1970s, when researchers in the physiology labs at UCLA explored the physiological effects of meditation techniques. This pioneering research on meditation was first published in *Scientific American, American Journal of Physiology,* and the journal *Science.*

teachers. Rather, he taught Buddhism, Zen, Jungian Psychology, and Ethics. During his classes, I first heard the colorful and entertaining term "Monkey Mind" – which is a mind that never rests and continually jumps from thought to thought, image to image. The Monkey Mind contributes to the perception of separation, the illusion that when we look around a room full of people, we see individuals separated by the space between them.

But the mind doesn't just jump from "tree to tree," it consistently analyzes and judges as well. The mind is like a butcher knife; it slices reality and cuts objects into easily comprehensible parts. Thus, at its most basic level, the mind's role is to separate the world into definable parts so that we may react appropriately to danger and decide whether to fight or take flight. Our reptilian brain triggers these self-preservation and survival instincts that are common to all animals. This is a fundamental reason why it is so difficult for us to see all of humanity as One.

Interestingly, if we could climb the layers of consciousness and reach Oneness, we might begin to disregard the line between life and death because at this level there's not much difference between the two. You might *perceive* yourself as the fire, the poisonous snake, the speeding bus ... so much so that you might run into the fire, hug the snake, or fall under the wheels of the bus.

In order to experience life beyond mere survival consciousness, attain deeper creativity and insight, and achieve a healthier, more balanced existence, we need to access a proven process for transitioning our minds to a higher state of awareness. One such process is meditation.

In the Eastern traditions, the first phase of meditation involves letting go of judgment and gradually reducing the amount of analysis, moving the mind toward the simpler act of witnessing/observing. Granted, this seems to be a paradox, since most people believe that the mind is a mechanism that is *supposed* to constantly think, measure, and analyze. You may as well tell your liver, "Stop filtering my blood; stop for just thirty minutes a day." Similarly, try saying to your heart, "I command you to stop pumping for thirty minutes."

Or try this exercise: Tell your mind to stop thinking about an elephant. As soon as you form that intention, your mind will either generate images or thoughts about elephants, and only elephants. Indeed, your mind will become obsessed with elephants!

Even when asleep, our minds analyze and jump around like curious monkeys. Yet, master teachers from the East maintain that we *can* tame the Monkey Mind using various methods of daily meditation. And these mental exercises accomplish more than just relaxing the mind: They create an incredible inner laboratory for healing mental and physical ills; they produce a practical tool for increasing imagination and creativity; and they chart a path to sacred ecstasy and Union!

Even Mozart, the most prolific composer in human history, experienced moments of "writer's block." When at a creative dead end, Mozart would drop down on his knees and pray – his meditative technique for clearing and centering the mind. After he was done praying, Mozart would go back to his desk to find musical ideas flowing once again, with the intensity and continuity of steady, blessed rain.

Mozart instinctively knew what the yogis of the East have observed for centuries – that meditation and prayer act to clear, calm, and refresh the wandering and restless mind. Meditation also provides us a chance for a new beginning. That clear and empty space is where an artist meets the muse and becomes inspired.[26]

Neurological research not only confirms that the yogis and Mozart had it right, scientific studies also show that, regardless of a person's faith or spiritual tradition, when he or she prays

---

26 See more on the subject of the muse and inspiration in Chapter XII, "The Mystery of Unplanned Creativity."

or meditates, there are several measurable changes that occur in the brain that result in lowered blood pressure, less stress and agitation, and reduced depression. These factors, in turn, result in a stronger immune system.[27]

Meditation, therefore, is a form of mental yoga that also impacts the physical body. The master yogis have proven that through long and dedicated meditation practice, one may control the mind, regulate internal organs, and even reach the profound state of *nirvana* (ultimate freedom).[28]

Ultimately, the goal of any meditation practice is to witness and experience the *yoga* (unity) of all being. At its highest and deepest level, meditation is similar to *Whadat* (union with the Beloved) achieved by the Sufis, and to the *Ichud* (unifying Oneness) experienced by the Hassidim. In sum, there are many paths to the Divine but the destination remains the same – Oneness. Paraphrasing the Sufi master Hazrat Inayat Khan:

There are many waves in the sea,
Yet they are all expressions of the One Great Ocean.
On the surface you see the waves.
A bit deeper you see they are all One Movement.

I invite you to try the meditation exercises detailed in Appendix B at end of this book. These exercises not only calm the mind and improve mental and physical health, they also represent the first stage of deeper spiritual work.

---

27 See *NeuroReport for Rapid Communication of Neuroscience Research* for articles on the neuroscience research of Professors Koelsch, Sammler, Bradt, Sarkamo, Rose, Kerer, and Soto.

28 See Paramhansa Yogananda's *Autobiography of a Yogi*, and the teachings of Sant Darshan Singh, Sant Kirpal Singh, and Sant Rajinder Singh.

وصلت مبارکی بنج نورشخ للة صدیق بلاد رض اللة واسعة الشرادی لاجرم نشکـه
دم اولدودی وهرکی بلاکهم ساعت قدد زیاده ملک اسنده عاسین بلردی مولا اصلی
بروبیدیم حال اوذب فراد ایغیم یم وشیبی مهلا اشده تابونی برشکاکر لاجوجه
ای کیتوزیب مدد سه بایللدلر دو مولا شمس لاندش باشین راوسی اودر نقوشبایده

(ب) لاقت مولانا ایندلا ایلم اودوس مزلم کوزدی امدنصکری رحلم نذکر ودم صوم ایله
ایم آی منزوی ایلم بیارک اسلام برزا اولخلوم لاسکرة قادا اولمردی ومعصام عقل بالشار
کم مولا لا شمس لادین جوینکیم قوینیم دیه کلوب مولا لا جاج اذلرلدیک خدمتنه کلدکده وقی
صله اوذره برحیسکـار له جاب والشار ایمدد رجب کتاب ذرکنه قوشلر یا جمرلزا

CHAPTER V

Shams' Last Teaching

By the time Jalaluddin Rumi reached his mid-thirties, he had not yet written one word of poetry. The poems that today lift up our spirits, advise us on how to live our lives, enrich our yoga classes, and light up so many concerts, spiritual conventions, interfaith events, weddings, funerals, and romantic outings … all of these were written by Rumi, but only after he met the man who would forever change his life: Shams of Tabriz.

Shams – which means "Sun" in Arabic – was a wandering sage, a strange monk from the central Asian city of Tabriz, who liked to appear, teach, and then disappear. This peculiar master was not fond of writing. He did not write down any of his lessons, nor would he let his students take notes. Rather, he would impart wisdom in a parable or two, stunning his listeners with gleaming beams of Light, and then he would disappear again, as was his custom to do.

One day Shams arrived in Konya, the home town of Rumi, who had escaped the Mongol massacres to become an outstanding Islamic scholar and philosopher in Anatolia.

There Rumi drew numerous students and followers of all tribes and faiths. They would forever call him "Mevlana."[29]

Both Shams and Rumi felt it was a blessed meeting that only the heavens could have convened. Here was the wise sage who disliked writing, searching to pour his first-hand knowledge of Divine wisdom into a vessel that could truly hold and channel it for years to come. And there was the great scholar, who had the potential to express in words the great mystery that is beyond *all* words, the great wisdom that is above *all* textbooks, intellect, or language. Shams possessed the teachings and Rumi carried within him the innate promise to put them into poems that could one day change the world.

And so the two masters fell into intense marathons of sacred conversation. Thereafter, Rumi began writing the astounding poetry that we read today, whether in its fully glorious Farsi verse or in its distilled English philosophical translations. Many of the poems have been credited to Shams, others have been credited to Rumi, but it was Rumi who composed the poems, entrusting them to his faithful assistants.

Yet, that paradise – the heaven-inspired dialogues between Shams and Rumi – lasted so long that some of Rumi's students began feeling rather neglected. Tension and jealousy ensued, until one day Shams disappeared, as was his custom to do. Rumi, left behind, was utterly destroyed.

He could not understand why Shams had left him! Especially now that Rumi had found his great spiritual guide: one to lead him toward the wisdom beyond all the facts he had memorized during his scholarly years, one to help him experience the ecstatic path toward the Light that penetrates all beings. Just as the blessing arrived, his master was gone.

Rumi could no longer sleep at night. Shams' disappearance was like an open wound in his heart. He could not comprehend it and could find no way to accept it.

---

29 "Our Master" in Turkish.

In the streets, people would whisper tantalizing rumors to Rumi: "Shams is in Samarkand" or "Someone saw him teaching near the pond at the Grand Mosque." Others would declare: "Shams is in Damascus" or "We saw him in the open market-place." And one informant boasted a particularly painful sighting: "I saw Shams playing chess with an Italian soldier named Francis who just returned from a bloody crusade to the Holy Land, and Shams is teaching him how to become the enlightened Saint of Assisi!"

"Rubbish! Complete nonsense!" interrupted another man with a low authoritative voice. "Mevlana, listen to me, Shams is dead – your students killed him and buried him!" But no one could find the body. There was no trace of Shams and no clues to follow …

Finally, Rumi decided to go and look for Shams himself, everywhere and anywhere he thought Shams might be. He traveled to each city that Shams had ever visited and to every village he may have gone, but still Shams was not to be found. Nobody had seen Shams, and Rumi had no more tidbits to follow.

Then one day Rumi arrived at the old marketplace in Damascus, where the spice merchants displayed their exotic goods by the woodworker shops and the big brass pot stands. In the midst of all the commotion, Rumi suddenly heard the voice of his master! He turned around, but there was no sign of Shams. He spun again, and then he saw him: *Shams was standing on the other side of the plaza with his back to Rumi.*

Hastily, Rumi ran toward Shams, grabbed him by the shoulder, and turned him around swiftly – but it was not Shams after all, just a man selling bread! Then he heard Shams' voice again, this time near the coffee grinder on the corner. He ran to the end of the street, but Shams was not there either!

Over and over again, Rumi heard Shams' voice around the hectic marketplace. From one end to the other and back again, he searched for Shams, turning and turning, round and round, hoping to catch a glimpse of his master. Faster and faster, Rumi spun, hearing Shams but not finding him, seeing Shams in his mind's eye but being unable to reach him with his arms.

Then – out of all the sounds of the crowded market – Rumi distinctly heard the piercing ring of the goldsmiths' hammers hitting the yellow metal: *tah, tah, tah, tah*. Now, Rumi circled even faster, turning and turning to the ringing which got louder and louder, as though the sound were emanating from inside his head. And all the while, he kept hearing Shams but not seeing him, seeing Shams but not finding him …

And then Rumi heard a new sound: Deep within the unending noise of the hammers hitting the gold – *tah, tah, tah, tah* – he recognized a sacred sound. He heard the holy name of the Breath of Life: *Allah, Allah, Allah!* And in complete ecstatic exhaustion, Rumi fell onto the ground in the central plaza of the old marketplace.

He then realized that his search was over. There was no need to look for Shams anymore. Shams had merged with his own being. There was no longer any need to look outside himself. Indeed, all the answers were right inside Rumi's heart, just as the sacred name of the Breath of Life, Allah, was hidden within the sound of the little metal hammers hitting pure gold: *tah, tah, tah, tah … Allah, Allah, Allah, Allah …*

This was the last teaching that Shams endowed upon the great Sufi master Mevlana Jalaluddin Rumi, who then went on to write the ecstatic poems that have inflamed the hearts of seekers and lovers of Truth with the living wisdom of his greatest mentor, Shams of Tabriz.

There are several legends recounting how Rumi met Shams of Tabriz and numerous tales on how Rumi began whirling, a sacred meditative and ecstatic movement ritual. The above story is only one of these, which I personally adore and have told during many of my concerts. My rendering of the above story typically leads into one of the Sufi Mevlevi songs that my ensemble plays for the whirling dervish during his turning ritual. Mevlevi – derived from the honorary title Mevlana – is the name of the order of Sufi dervishes that Rumi's son Sultan Walad established after his father's passing. Today, the Mevlevi Museum and Rumi's mausoleum are located in Konya, Turkey.[30]

In 2011, I led a group of forty-five supporters of the Yuval Ron Ensemble to Konya. While there, we were most fortunate to be greeted and hosted by the gracious Mevlevi leader Jelaleddin Loras, who invited me to participate in the Sufi Sema (whirling) ritual at the dervishes' school. Sheikh Loras kindly insisted that I open the evening with an oud solo and lead a local ensemble into the first song.[31] Playing with these masterful Mevlevi musicians throughout the rest of the night, experiencing the ritual with the Sufi dervishes in the home of their Sheikh, while being in the city where Rumi himself had lived his incredibly inspired life eight hundred years ago, was one of the highlights of my life.

---

30 Sadly, the Mevlevi Order was outlawed by the Republic of Turkey in 1925. Partial rights have been restored to permit performance of dervish ceremonies in public.

31 Please see the Yuval Ron Ensemble video *Seeker of Truth* (DVD) (www. cdbaby.com/cd/theyuvalronensemble) for more information and music related to my work with the whirling dervishes and Sufi music teachings.

С. Викилзванни
2001

CHAPTER VI

Master of the Good Name

Every baby is a special baby. Every life is special. But once, many years ago in a small village in far away Ukraine, an *extraordinarily* special baby was born, and his parents called him Yisrael.

Shortly after Yisrael was born, his father died, and then his mother, too. The people of the village all realized that they would have to take care of this little boy, who was now the responsibility of the community. And so, everybody fed, took care of, and gave little Yisrael as much love as they could possibly give. They raised him well, and when he turned six years old, they sent him to the village school.

But that little child, that Yisrael, was different than all the other kids in the school. While the other children were learning the alphabet, little Yisrael was looking outside the window, watching the birds and listening to their singing. While all the other children were memorizing names and formulas, little Yisrael was watching the wild dance of the leaves that were blown away by the cold autumn wind outside the window.

Then one day, the principal called Yisrael to the office and announced to him that the school had just lost all hope in his ability to study. Therefore, the principal had no choice but to advise Yisrael to stay home and give up his schooling.

However, instead of staying home, little Yisrael went to the forest. And while the other kids learned to read and write, this little boy learned to distinguish the tracks of wild rabbits, coyotes, and wolves. He studied the various bird calls and taught himself to sing along with the tapping rhythm of the soft snow flakes which fell down on the wet ground in early spring. He memorized the various sounds of wind blowing through the trees, and he could tell the difference between the poisonous plants and the medicinal herbs. The forest was his academy.

On the day he turned fifteen, Yisrael reappeared at the village school. He went right to the principal's office – the same principal who had kicked him out years ago – and said, "I am now ready to teach in your school. Would you please assign me to one of the classrooms?"

Astounded, the principal also was delighted and relieved, because he knew it had been the responsibility of the community to raise this child and for a very long time he harbored guilt, feeling that he failed badly when he expelled Yisrael from school. Now, as the boy stood in front of him in his office, a joyful thought leapt into the principal's mind: *It is the Holy Name himself that sent this peculiar boy back to me so that I could correct my ways!* And so he said to Yisrael with a tender voice, "Come near my boy, I simply cannot assign you to be a classroom teacher at this time, but I do have a job for you. Each morning you will escort the students from their homes to school and at the end of the day from school back to their homes."

Yisrael replied joyfully, "This is just what I wanted."

And so the next day, Yisrael escorted the children to school. But all the kids were very, very late to school because Yisrael took a long detour through the forest, where he had all the children singing with the birds, dancing among the leaves that were blown by the forest wind, and building fairy houses for the angels and spirits of the night. And the same thing happened the following morning, and again the next day, and the days following that.

One would think that the parents, the teachers and the principal would soon protest, but no! They all realized with much surprise that the children were doing better in school. The kids were doing better in math, with their readings, and on their spelling tests. They all did their homework in half the time as usual, received better grades than before, and enjoyed deeper and more peaceful sleep. All in all, they were healthier and happier children.

Thus, Yisrael gained the people's respect. Eventually the Rabbi himself matched Yisrael with the sweetest young lady of the village. Soon after the wedding and to everyone's surprise, Yisrael took his young wife and a few books and abruptly left the village.

It was a time of secluded study in the mountains, where Yisrael immersed himself in old Kabbalistic books that he had gotten from Spain. For many years he contemplated ancient formulas and mystical systems of the Jewish esoteric tradition, until he finally felt ready. Then he took his wife and kids, descended from the mountains, and returned to the community, where he began making miracles!

By chanting various mystical names of God, Yisrael was able to heal people. He used the power of sound and mystical teaching to bring blessings to the world. From then on he became known as the "Baal Shem Tov" ("Master of the Good Name").

The big idea the Baal Shem introduced two hundred and fifty years ago is that we *can* join with the Source of Life and unite with the Absolute that exists everywhere, yet can be seen nowhere. How could that be? This omnipresent force is a riddle that even the world's best scientists have yet to figure out ... and they may never, ever solve this divine puzzle. There are no words to adequately explain it, yet the Baal Shem taught that we can try to join with this energy through *music, dance,* and *joy.*[32]

And so, the Baal Shem Tov established a musical tradition of melodies that have no lyrics. He knew all too well that music engages the mysteries beyond all words and awakens the heart. When we insert language into our music or meditation, we are bound to engage our intellect – and that is exactly what we do *not* want to do when exploring the Reality beyond all realities.

Therefore, many of the devotional songs from this tradition are sung in gibberish, like "bim, bam, bim, bim, bam" or "lei, lei, oye." And by repeating these sounds and accelerating their pace, we have the potential to travel from the pain of separation to the joy of unity. We can lose ourselves in fiery excitement, stepping outside of ourselves and letting our soul rise up to dance with the Master of the Universe, the Creator of the divine drama that we call ... LIFE![33]

---

32 For further discussion on the practice of ecstatic joyful union through music and dance see Chapter II, "Sacred Ecstasy."

33 This imaginative retelling of the story of the Baal Shem Tov first came to me during a TED talk I gave in California in 2010. At the end of my talk, one of the leading scientists in the room came to me and said with enthusiastic voice, "You are right! The future of science is beyond books and dry facts. The new frontier of scientific exploration of the many remaining mysteries of the universe is within the realm of mystics and artists, namely the path of intuition!" You can see Yuval's TED Talk at: www.youtube.com/watch?v=ZgTE1VJxaCQ.

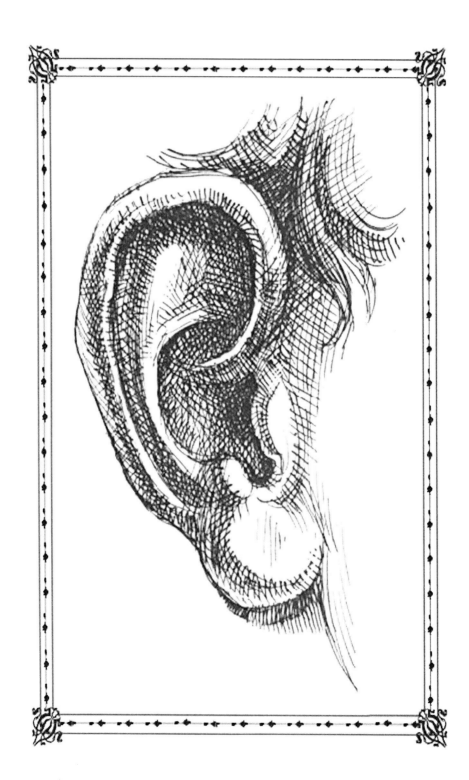

CHAPTER VII

The Power of a Little Tune

Life is a divine theater. Today, as in every day, the One is playing hide-and-seek with humanity. And in this continuous, interactive play, those who are unable to see the Oneness of all things put up numerous barriers in order to divide their reality, to create a sense of identity, to protect illusions, and to calm fears. We see such divisions everywhere – within all societies, religions, work places, institutions, and even within families. However, sometimes great tragedies bring people back together so that they may again sense the Oneness that we all share. Sometimes it is merely a little tune, a few musical notes, that magically build a bridge over difficult waters.

"I wish I could see him in real life!" Moni used to tell me. He never met his grandfather but always felt his grandfather's presence within his own inner being – in the background behind his thoughts and emotions. Moni used to imagine his grandfather's raspy voice rising above the holiday table when all the cousins and family members would gather around for the special Passover dinner on *Leil Haseder*.[34] His grandfather was an East European rabbi who escaped to the ancient Hebrew homeland before the darkest days of the Second World War.

Moni's father would often tell him about Saba Shmulik, the grandfather he never met.[35] "Saba Shmulik loved his kids more than the entire world! And he loved singing little tunes they called *Nigunim*.[36] He would sing these tunes with no words except for random sounds such as 'bim, bam, yam, bam, lai, lai, and oye.'"

Moni's father grew up in Israel in a Polish-Jewish family which immigrated to the first Hebrew city built on the desert dunes. Yet, they preferred to live in the past: They held on to their old East European Yiddish tongue[37] and sweated under the hot sun, wearing black suits, heavy hats and coats, just like they used to wear during the freezing-cold Polish winters. Saba Shmulik liked to say that they "lived in the past in order to carry

---

34 *Leil Haseder* is the first night of Passover when a ritualistic festive meal is offered to commemorate the exodus of the Hebrew slaves out of Egypt.

35 *Saba* in Hebrew means "grandfather."

36 *Nigunim* are songs without words used by Hassidic Jewish communities in East Europe and composed by their spiritual leaders, starting with the mystical master Baal Shem Tov, the founder of the Hassidic movement. Literally "tunes," these *nigunim* are meant to engage the heart and soul, rather than the intellect. The Hassidim sing these tunes at weddings, holidays and worship, and the songs sometimes lead to a sacred ecstatic experience. For more on this practice see Chapter II, "Sacred Ecstasy."

37 Yiddish, which was at one time the international language of the Jews of Central and Eastern Europe and their descendants, is a hybrid of Hebrew and medieval German.

their heritage into the future, for the sake of the children and for the sake of the Hebrew tribes of Moses, King David, and the prophets."

But Moni's father had a different viewpoint. He was the youngest child and the *only* one who was born in this new yet ancient homeland, and for that reason he always felt estranged from his family. In fact, he admired anything Arabic: Bedouins,[38] camels, oud music, and most of all, the soft, sandy desert dunes. He was attracted to anything and everything that grew out of that desert. The European customs his Polish Jewish mother forced on the children, as well as the foods, always felt foreign to Moni's father. He loved the simple pleasures of eating humus in a pita, of dipping fresh sesame bagel into *zaatar*[39] held in small, recycled newspaper pieces, and walking by the falafel stands on the streets, where they served fried potatoes on top of a pita stuffed with fresh salad and tahini sauce.

From a young age, Moni's father disliked wearing the layers of black and white clothing and a head-cover, rebelling against grandfather Saba Shmulik by wearing mostly shorts, t-shirts, and biblical sandals. He also detested reciting the daily prayers, which to him seemed merely an automatic and rapid mumbling routine. More tragically for the family, Moni's father ended up marrying a dark-skinned Iraqi-born Jewish woman, who was completely secular and anti-religious and who also loved anything Bedouin.

After the young couple ran away and wed, the family considered Moni's father a dead man. He had crossed too many lines. But one day a year, on Passover for *Leil Haseder*, Moni's father would be allowed back into the grandfather's house. At the end of the festive dinner, Saba Shmulik would call all of the male cousins and uncles to gather around him. They all were dressed in their Orthodox Jewish black and white uniforms,

---

38 Nomads of Arabic Muslim ethnicity who live in the Middle Eastern desert.

39 A mix of fresh Mediterranean thyme, sesame seeds, sumac, and salt.

standing apart from Moni's father, who wore his usual, simple white shirt and pants. Then Saba Shmulik would point to his son, Moni's father, and say to all the cousins and uncles around: "You see him? He may look different than all of you, but remember, he has the same *neshama* as you. He has the same soul. Remember this!"[40]

Many years passed. Moni was attending the School of Near East Studies when he got a call that his father had been taken to the hospital. They said it was his heart. And Moni *knew* – as he rushed into the hospital room – that his father was on his deathbed. Moni sat down next to the bed and put his hand over his father's chest. His father was still breathing, but his eyes were closed in exhaustion.

Then, out of nowhere, there was a knock at the door. Moni looked up and saw a man dressed in black and white with a fur hat on his head, sweating in the mid-summer heat. It was his uncle, whom he had met only once in his life, his father's brother who would never ever step foot in Moni's family home. This man in black walked into the hospital room and said nothing.

The uncle looked at Moni, looked at his dying estranged brother, and moved slowly toward the bed. He grabbed a chair in an awkward manner and sat down, right next to his brother's head. Moni looked at his uncle, the uncle looked at Moni's father, and then his uncle moved his lips near to the dying man's ear. Then Moni heard a voice – a shaky, soft, East European male voice – slowly mumble a little tune from a faraway town in Eastern Europe, a simple tune with no words. This gibberish combined with a few simple notes ascended slowly and gradually, a peculiar mixture of sadness and potential joy. The uncle was singing a *nigun* in his brother's ear …

---

40 In Hebrew, *neshama* means "soul." In Kabbalistic terminology, it represents the Divine spark, which each living thing carries inside.

Moni's father opened his eyes, looked at Moni, and gazed at the ceiling. For a moment, it was as if his eyes whispered to an empty space above his bed, "I know." Then he closed his eyes and took his last breath.

The uncle stood up, turned around, and slowly walked out of the room, without saying a word.

Since that day, the tune his uncle sang lingered deep inside Moni's mind. It kept on playing again and again, until Moni knew it by heart. He even heard it in his sleep, and in a strange way, he began to associate his late father's memory with that *nigun*, a simple tune from the old country, a cold East European town, far away from the sandy desert dunes.

A few years later, Moni got a call from a cousin who left him a message at work. The message said that his uncle was sick and in the hospital – the very uncle who had come to see his dying father was now lying in a hospital room himself. And although Moni hated hospitals and funerals, he felt an irresistible force inside of him pushing him forward, toward the door, and outside to the street. He then found himself running by foot to that hospital, the same terrible hospital where his father had passed away several years back.

Moni entered the hospital and reached the room where his uncle was lying, half dead/half alive. He pushed open the door to see a room full of people. They were all his cousins. Nine men seated around the bed – all pale, holding prayer books, swaying forward and backward in intense prayer.

Moni entered the room and said nothing. The old man was lying on the bed with his eyes closed. His chest was not moving and he already looked dead. The cousins stared at Moni. He felt out of place wearing his t-shirt, short pants, and sandals, surrounded by his nine cousins who were dressed in their East European black suits and headcovers, all sweating in the oppressive summer heat.

Suddenly, from within, Moni felt something urging him to move toward his uncle's bed. It was as if somebody else was inside him, pushing him toward his dying uncle, forcing him to lean down and press his lips close to his uncle's ear.

The nine cousins froze like ice sculptures, as they stared at Moni in a confused gaze of fear and wonder. And then they heard a voice, a shaky weak voice that began to hum an old tune. Moni was singing a little *nigun* from a faraway East European Jewish town, the same one his uncle had sung to Moni's father on his deathbed. Moni sang with his eyes closed. And the *nigun* poured out of him in spite of himself. He sang for the uncle, for his late father, and for his grandfather Saba Shmulik, whom he never met.

Then, to the cousins' astonishment, their father opened his eyes. The old man was listening to the *nigun*, and it seemed as if he were drinking it in, like medicinal syrup. First, he saw Moni. Then he looked around the room at his nine sons, all pallid and stunned. It was as if a miracle had occurred!

The old man then lifted his head from the pillow and pointed to Moni with a trembling finger. "You see him? He may look different than all of you, but remember, he has the same *neshama* as you. He has the same soul. Remember this!"

Then Moni's uncle lay back down, sank his head into the pillow, and took his last breath.

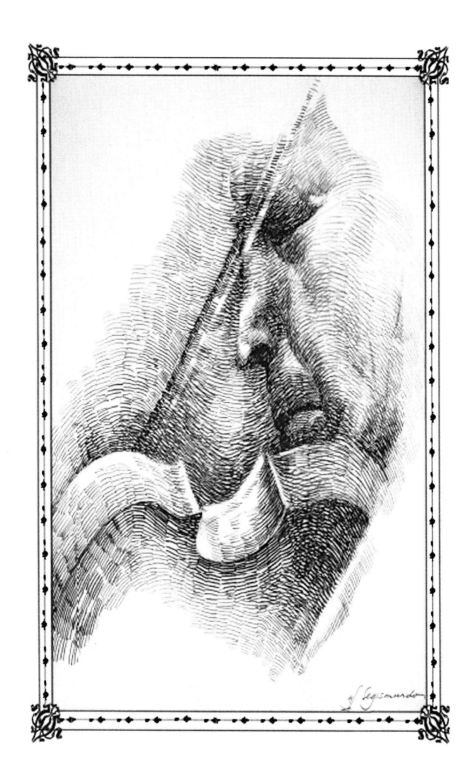

Chapter VIII

On the Nature of
Harmonious Sound and Beauty

Often I have been asked to speak about "Music and the Sacred" or "Music and Spirituality." It is an endless exploration. Indeed, the more one contemplates the nexus between music and the Divine, the more one becomes aware of the vast and fascinating nature of these themes.

Years of researching various spiritual traditions have led me to deeply appreciate and experience first-hand how music excels in evoking emotions and altered states of consciousness. I also have become intimate with the power of music and sound through studying the art of film scoring and the science of psycho-acoustics, and through working as a composer for film, TV, theater, and contemporary dance.

Imagine trying to express the feeling of awe that is experienced when we commune with something greater than ourselves. The original vibration or emotion that the soul feels must then be transformed by the brain into a word, a description, or an intellectual idea – which may or may not create a similar vibration in an audience. Often the strength of the original emotion is diminished in the process, and the reader or listener receives a muted or weaker vibration. Such a "conversion" may pale in comparison to our original feeling of awe, the original *inaudible* vibration that we feel in our heads, in our bellies, or in our hearts. Therefore, I consider words to be a mere translation of an inner vibration. And it is often the same when translating literature: The resulting byproduct, in most cases, is weaker than the source.

On the other hand, the reader or listener may carry powerful associations, connotations, or memories which are awakened by a certain word that causes a strong inner vibration. These personal reactions may reinforce the otherwise muted vibration of the written or audible word.

Take for instance the word "blood." When you read it, many personal associations may come alive inside of you, thereby initiating secondary inner vibrations which you may interpret as emotions. The writer likely intended to awaken some of these responses, while other feelings were never even imagined by the author, having been brought in through the personal experience of the reader. This is the magic of literature, especially poetry.

With music, on the other hand, I can express an emotion or vision *directly* into a sound wave which immediately affects the listener's mental and physical state. Consequently, music is a very powerful form of communication and therapy, because its initial impact is *not* intellectual, as in the case of language. Rather, in its most immediate stage, the "magical" phenomenon of music actually side-steps the intellect. It vibrates your eardrums, your bones, your tissues, your nervous system, and your brain. Your mental processes of abstract analysis and interpretation will be triggered only after the sound is initially experienced on a vibrational level. That is what sets music apart from literary arts.

Indeed, it is difficult to describe this initial vibrational experience. People who have attended my concerts often tell me some amazing yet vague descriptions of what they experienced, such as: "I felt something move inside of me ... I felt something very sacred ... I felt something greater than myself."

Yuval Ron at a musical retreat creating soul-stirring vibrations

Music has the power to bring about such reactions because music is a complex, artistic, creative set of vibrations. And when it reaches the listener, that array of sound waves vibrates the *whole* human being – body *and* soul.

People respond differently to various sound vibrations based on the frequency (i.e., whether the pitch is high or low), the strength of the vibration (i.e., volume), the pulsation rate of the vibration (i.e., rhythm), and the way various vibrations (tones) and rhythms are combined (i.e., composition, which is a central part of the art of music). There are various combinations of musical vibrations, referred to as "modes" and "chords," which can lead the listener to feel a vast range of emotions, including melancholia, nostalgia, hopefulness, or agitation. Since ancient times, these combinations have been utilized by many cultures to enhance medical treatments (early forms of music therapy), military operations (such as the drums and bugle), and nearly all religious ceremonies. In recent times, music has been used to dramatically manipulate the emotions of movie theater audiences.[41]

Thus, like the tribal shaman, the art of a composer, the art of a musician is to *master* the use of these various sound vibrations and their effects. Each time I sit to play in front of an audience and every time I sit to compose music for films or other art forms, I am reminded of the powerful impact of music on the emotional states and perceptions of audiences.

I remember the very first time I strummed the guitar. When I heard the plain strings simply vibrating, it sounded *so* beautiful to me. Yet, it was nothing much, not even a musical composition. And it certainly was not a well-crafted Mozart symphony or a masterful Beatles song. It was *simply* the open strings of the guitar strummed by a first-time student. But, I thought to myself: *Wow – that is beautiful!*

The musical experience of beauty also is based on harmony or harmonious sounds and vibrations. At the tender age of eleven, I heard the simple harmony of the open strings of the guitar during my first guitar lesson, and the sound drew me in. I experienced a moment of harmony coming out of my own fingers, and I sensed I could produce even greater beauty with the most basic of elements.

We tend to associate the term "beauty" with a narrow category of visual images that aesthetically please us. For example, when I see a gorgeous flower in the garden, it often leads to some inner sense of pleasure. I then resort to using the word "beautiful" in an attempt to express and release what

---

41 For more on the fascinating abilities of music and sound to affect human emotions, see Chapter X, "The Vanishing Modes."

I am feeling. People often visit a museum, point to some object and say, "This is such a beautiful sculpture." That usually is an indication that they have been visually stimulated by an aesthetic arrangement of elements in space which has caused feelings of pleasure. Sound, on the other hand, is a different type of "beauty" – a vibrational pleasure, which some people find to be a deeper and longer lasting experience than that created by visual stimulation.

In mystical terms, the phenomenon of "beauty" is associated with the quest for "truth." In several spiritual traditions, such as Islam, "Truth" is one of the names or attributes of the Creator. If you follow this perspective, beauty becomes a much grander term, often describing the state of harmony which is achieved when we are in accord with the All that cannot be denied.

When I refer to this harmony, I mean aspects which work together in concert but which also may exist within some state of conflict, paradox, or contradiction, thereby mirroring the complexity and reality of creation. The world *is* in harmony, but there are always conflicts within it. Just take a look inside our bodies. As we speak, inside every healthy, harmonious body, there are "good" immune system cells attacking "bad" bacteria cells. This battle keeps the number of bodily invaders under control, and there are several such fights going on inside each one of us.

The same is true with a great piece of music or art. Within every musical masterpiece, there are some conflicting melodic lines, moments of tension and possibly dark or "ugly" moments (i.e., dissonant or discordant). However, the work as a whole balances the "good" and the "bad," the accordant and the discordant, the tension and its release, and striking that balance is the key to achieving a harmonic constellation and producing music that is "beautiful."

Thus, beauty is produced by – or rather through – a master artist or anyone who is an effective conduit for creative energy. Whether artists are aware of it or not, when they create or interpret an inspired work, they are in fact allowing themselves to become an instrument or a vehicle for a higher creative power. They then become a tool in the service of a greater spirit, as are the paintbrush, the potting wheel, the violin strings.

But, who is flowing through the artist, choosing the paint colors, manipulating the clay, moving the bow along the strings?[42] Many artists call it "inspiration," a "muse," or God, depending on the term they like. They may not even be aware that by simply crediting inspiration, they *are* acknowledging a power at work that is greater than they, themselves.[43] Researching the mysterious nature of that power and the process of creativity may contribute to our understanding of the source of all life. Thus far, science has provided little insight into this enigma, as scientists have yet to unveil the locus of inspiration. As one leading neurologist admitted, the current level of scientific understanding of the process of creativity is "poor at best."[44]

I believe that when we create, we channel some higher source, something greater than ourselves. We actually express this every day without noticing, as when we hear a great piece of music and think: *Wow, that is beautiful... that artist is inspired!* What we are saying in these instances, even if not consciously, is that *spirit* is *in* the artist ("inspiration" = "in-spirit"). Moreover, we are saying that the artist takes in a breath of life (another mystical definition of the Creator). Therefore, we realize – on at least a subliminal level – that there is a duet here,

---

42 Paraphrased from the poem "In the Stillness of Your Depth," in *Book of Hours,* by Reiner Maria Rilke. Yuval Ron's rendition of the poem appears on the CD *Rilke: Searching for the Inner Soul*, which is translated and read by Mark Robert Waldman and accompanied by original music composed by Yuval Ron (www.cdbaby.com/cd/ronwaldman).

43 See a discussion of inspiration, the muse, and the mysteries of the creative process in Chapter XII, "The Mystery of Unplanned Creativity."

44 A quote from a TED talk by Charles Limb, M.D., researcher of music, creativity and the brain at Johns Hopkins University.

a dance between a skilled and masterful artist and a mysterious higher power (i.e., spirit, breath of life, muse, divinity, the Tao, or whatever name we put to it).

But as much as the artist is involved in shaping and channeling the work of art, beauty also is created *randomly*. In other words, beauty may come about with little or no human control. Let's look at nature as a prime example. We easily can see in the wild how breathtaking beauty is created via a perpetual process that some call the Tao – an all encompassing flow that may at first blush appear random, but which has intelligible patterns and is therefore beyond randomness.[45]

In Western art, a "random" process for creating music and dance was developed in the 1960s and it was called "Chance Operation." Influenced by Zen Buddhism, American composer John Cage would order the orchestra conductor and performers to throw dice in order to determine the notes or the musical beats of his compositions. Cage wanted to relinquish control and highlight the invisible role of randomness, chance, the Supreme Being, the Divine (or whatever name you prefer). It was Cage's way of inviting people to entertain the questions: *Who is creating? Who is the real artist? Are we in control of the creative process? Or are we a conduit for higher power?* In that sense, "randomness" is the artist's co-creator; it flows and dances with the artist during the process of creating a work of art, of bringing forth beauty.

In Japanese, the word "music" is made up of two characters: "noise" and "pleasure." In other words, Japanese culture allows any noise or sound to be considered music, provided that it pleases some listener. If one is enjoying the sound of raindrops falling on a tin roof, that sound *is* music! Once again, the question becomes: *Who is the composer?* Regardless of the answer, that

---

45   The Tao is an ancient Chinese philosophy which espouses the "Way" (literally, "watercourse way"), a formless, supreme power, which is the source of all things and which allows us to create without effort and without over-powering the resulting artistic creation.

sound – according to Japanese logic – is art, and hearing that sound is experiencing beauty.

Lastly, we need beauty in order to feed our souls. Beauty nurtures us. When we experience beautiful art, when we experience a beautiful moment in nature, we feel better, we feel reenergized, we feel inspired. It is as if life energy suddenly is pumped inside us. Without beauty, everything around us would seem gray. Incidentally, if you place the average person in a gray office, with all gray furniture, a gray carpet, gray walls and gray computers, after a couple of months he or she will become depressed – just as the average person would become depressed if deprived of sunlight.

For me, beauty is as necessary as sunlight, and experiencing beauty brings a certain dance into my soul. It vibrates the core of my being and makes me feel truly alive!

Artists, in particular, have the power to transform ugliness into beauty. Imagine a sculptor taking pieces of rusted iron and arranging them in such a way that a sculpture, a work of art, suddenly emerges. As if by magic, unattractive chunks of metal give us pleasure because of their harmonious composition in space. Hence, the artist has elevated seemingly ugly and unpleasant materials (substitute discordant sounds, in the case of music) into art, beauty, and truth. This has been our role as artists.

Yet, the power to transform the world through art is not limited to artists alone. Nearly everyone has the means to help remodel a deteriorating neighborhood or simply paint their home and surround it with harmonious vegetation or luscious fruit trees. Projecting such beauty within their communities can provide another point of light in this world. Regardless of how small this light may be, it is another contribution of beauty, harmony, and positive energy to help elevate and reorient the physical world toward a unifying spiritual field.

Truly, every human being has a role in creating beauty, whether it is in the arts, farming, social work, medicine, education, waste management, or even banking! Each one of us is meant to continuously create. And we do this by embarking on a journey to discover our own unique way of elevating our world and each other. Then, life itself becomes art – art for the sake of co-creating a better and more beautiful planet, a healthier and more harmonious existence.

These days, I hear about this quest for a positive change everywhere I go. Surely, this is sign of a shifting consciousness in response to the worsening conditions of our planet. But this is not a new concept. For generations, Jewish tradition has referred to it as *Tikkun Olam* – the repair of the world, the repair of the environment, and the repair of humanity. And *that* is the meaning of life!

CHAPTER IX

Rumi, Najara, and the Dancing Camels

I am familiar with two mystical legends about the impact of music on camels. I have retold these stories during many of my talks on the use of the musical modes in the Middle East. The first tale comes from the dervish tradition of the Mevlevi Sufi Order, the other from the Sephardic Jewish heritage of the mystical city of Tzfat. Both feature great sages who were deeply involved in music and mysticism: the earlier master being Mevlana Jalaluddin Rumi, and the later mystic being Rabbi Israel Najara. I trust their spirits would be delighted to see their legacies woven together in this chapter.

The great mystic poet Rumi had immense love for the ney reed flute. To Rumi, his flute was more than a musical instrument. It was an ever-present metaphor for a human being: cut off at birth from the source, put into the fire of life, and drilled with holes of experience to finally become a perfect vessel for the breath of life. And Rumi knew that in the height of such a journey, a person could transcend being a mere channel, ultimately becoming an instrument for creating beauty, channeling music and poetry, and expressing a myriad of emotions, such as love, joy, wonder, longing, and pain.

One day Rumi sat down with his ney to have a warm cup of chai beside the colorful spice stand in the outdoor market of Konya. Soon, many of his students gathered around him, asking questions about life, death, and some blasphemous words they heard Shams – the eccentric sage of Tabriz – shouting around the market the day before.[46]

"Shams says that instead of going on the sacred pilgrimage to the Kaaba at Mecca, we ought to circle a poor man seven times and then give him our money," whispered a redheaded, Christian-Greek dervish who had been dutifully following Rumi's teachings for many years.

Rumi paused then picked up his ney and inhaled a long breath. He closed his eyes and exhaled very slowly through the reed. One wavy tone came out of the ney and enveloped the circle of pupils who filled the narrow alleyway. Rumi kept on blowing, but all that sounded was a single continuous note. And that breathy, wide, long note seemed to calm the inquisitive and somewhat agitated group of students.

---

46 Shams was a wandering sage from the city of Tabriz in Central Asia who became Rumi's spiritual teacher and confidant. You can read more on the legendary relationship between Shams and Rumi in Chapter V, "Shams' Last Teaching."

Finally, Rumi separated his lips from the ney, opened his eyes and said, "Do not listen to Shams. *That* is my role. Your task is to listen to no one but me! Turn around your heart. The sacred rock is in there. Your heart is the Temple, and that's where the Master of the Universe resides."

"Would we find the Master of the Universe even in the heart of an animal, let's say within the beating heart of a camel?" inquired one of the Jewish students with a slightly cynical and somewhat philosophical tone.

Rumi smiled. "Go fetch your camels. Bring along seven of them. Then lock them up in the old washroom and pour seven bags of salt over the stone floor. Give them no food or water for three days and three nights. And then we shall meet again for an observation."

"Most bizarre," thought the students, but they were obedient dervishes and promptly fulfilled their Master's instructions to the smallest detail.

On the fourth day, the students met Mevlana[47] at the washroom. They could hear the poor camels' cries. For three days and three nights the beasts had been licking the salty floor, searching for food and water, and in desperation they had grown thirstier and thirstier without end.

"Take the camels to the river bed and let them drink the good sweet water," ordered Rumi. "Go right to the water with no delay whatsoever!"

The dervishes hurriedly followed Rumi's orders, and in their urgent plight none of them noticed that Mevlana Rumi had disappeared from all sight.

As the strange caravan of thirsty camels and curious seekers arrived at the riverbank, they heard a most enchanting sound.

---

47 *Mevlana* means "our Master" in Turkish, from which came the word *Mevlevi* – a follower of Mevlana Rumi.

It was the cry of the ney. Rumi was sitting on a rock in the middle of the water playing the ney, exploring one of the most mystical musical modes of the Middle East.[48]

The young dervishes stood transfixed by the riverbank. The poor camels, recently freed from the salty jail, completely disregarded the sweet water. Without stopping to drink, all seven of the thirsty camels began slowly walking through the water toward the crying ney. It was as if the beasts were hypnotized, forgetting all thirst or desire, marching straight toward Rumi like metal shreds being pulled through space by a powerful magnet.

The great sage fixed his gaze on the camels as he kept playing the enchanted, ornamented improvisation. And just as the camels reached the middle point between the riverbank and the rock, Rumi smoothly changed the musical mode. The cry of the ney morphed into a ray of hope. Immediately, all seven camels stopped walking and began, with great delight, to drink the sweet water.

Rumi smiled at the dervishes. "You see, the cry of the ney travels and impacts all hearts and all living things. Wherever you turn, there is the Heart of the Universe. Turn, turn and you will see. Allow the music to expand your heart, and the sound will take you to the Beloved."

---

48 For more on the nature of the musical modes of the Middle East and their effect on culture and psychology, see Chapter X, "The Vanishing Modes."

Rabbi Najara[49] loved the sound of the shepherd's flute echoing off the green mountains around the Sea of Galilee. There was one spot on the highest mountain where he could hear a special tone echoing from above and below. It was as if the higher worlds and the lower worlds were sending back numerous reflections of the sound. *"Ya Ribon Olam!"* exclaimed Rabbi Najara. "Master of the Universe and all the worlds, you are the King of kings, you are in all creation, everywhere I look!" The birds sang back to him with a joyful tune and seemed to agree with his perception.

Najara was the son of a Spanish Jewish family that had been thrown out of Spain after living there six hundred years because – according to the Queen of Spain – they followed a "bad form of faith." But nothing could break the belief of young Najara. There was not enough darkness and pain to put out the Light that he saw everywhere he looked. And so, Najara dedicated his life to composing hundreds of songs and poems praising the Holy Name, the One which is the Creator of the Universe.

One day Rabbi Najara was on the side of the mountain just outside the old, stone-paved town of Tzfat.[50] His students and friends were resting during the early afternoon break, but Najara was with the birds and sheep, writing poems out in the fields. He was so entranced with the words that were flowing through his mind that he neglected to be aware of what was transpiring around him. Slowly but surely, he was surrounded

---

49 Rabbi Israel Najara was a son of a Jewish family that was expelled from Spain in 1492 and settled in Damascus, Syria. Najara, who was known as a talented poet and songwriter, moved to the mystical city of Tzfat, which today is located in northern Israel. His sacred poems and songs have enjoyed great popularity among the Jewish communities of the Near East and North Africa. He was the first to publish a book of sacred Jewish songs containing references to the origin of the melodies used for these songs – some from Arabic, others from Ottoman Turkish sources.

50 Tzfat originally was located in the northern end of the ancient Kingdom of Israel.

by a gang of thieves, young men from the neighboring village, sons of nomad tribes that wandered north from the desert, many years past. The thieves grabbed Najara without a word, tied him on top of their horse, and with their camels riding behind, they disappeared over the horizon.

All the while, Rabbi Najara hummed a new poem: "All the Great Name does in the world, is for the good." He was still chanting these words to himself when the thieves took him into a dark cave and searched him fully. After they discovered he had no valuables or any coins, they resolved to kill him right there so no witness would be left behind.

Rabbi Najara – who truly thought that it was the will of the Master of the Universe to have him return to the higher worlds at that moment – asked humbly for his last wish. "Please people, before I die, please let me play just one last simple shepherd tune on my beloved flute."

The thieves sat down, took out bread and olives and said, "Go ahead and play a tune for us while we eat, and then, it will be your time to die!"

Rabbi Najara closed his eyes, took the flute out from his pocket, put it to his lips, and waited to hear some sound, some tone from inside of him. He waited, listening intently, but there was no sound and no tune in his head, just words. Like a mantra, the words kept circling in his mind: *All that the Great Name does in the world is for good. All that the Great Name does in the world is for good.*

Then all of a sudden, the words vanished – there was nothing. Najara had no idea how long that "nothing" lasted, but finally he *did* hear a tone in his head. He tried with honest intention to blow that very same note through his flute, and he played it just right! And so he followed along and played another note and another … until a melody erupted, a joyful simple folk dance tune he never had heard before. Najara kept on playing the melody faster and faster, with great wonder at his immense feat.

He then witnessed the most incredible sight: The camels, the beasts of these thieves, started stepping to the beat of his tune. The camels were dancing! And Najara continued playing the bouncy tune until the thieves noticed that something unusual was unfolding.

"Why is this idiot so happy?" said one of the thieves, who stood up quickly with slight suspicion and a bit of amusement. The other thieves pulled knives from their belts and then they saw it too: Their camels, their good old, well-trained wild camels, were dancing joyfully to the beat of the flute!

"Run away from him, he is a sorcerer!" screamed one thief.

"He is a dangerous man, he is controlling our camels!" shouted another.

"He bewitched our camels. Run for your lives!" demanded the leader. And with no delay, all the thieves ran out of the cave, as if the whole world were collapsing on their heads.

But Najara did not even notice. Completely ecstatic, he danced with his precious flute, repeating again and again the little happy tune that had just saved his life. And he kept on playing his flute, as he walked back to Tzfat with the dancing camels hopping behind him all the way home.

To this very day, the people of Tzfat still carry the memory of this incredible sight. They have been telling this amazing legend of Rabbi Najara and the dancing camels to everyone they know – their family, friends, and guests. Indeed, they have been retelling this curious story and keeping Najara's devotional songs alive for over four hundred years.[51]

---

51 The Yuval Ron Ensemble's rendition of Rabbi Najara's tune "Ya Ribbon Olam" is available on the CD *Seeker of Truth*, Track 2, "Ya Rab El Alam" ("Master of the Universe") (www.cdbaby.com/cd/yuval9).

CHAPTER X

The Vanishing Modes

A distant sound of a Muslim prayer met with a loud chiming of a church bell. Although coming from afar, the ornamental and pleading sound of the mosque's call for prayer dominated the air ...

I was in the old city of Jerusalem, holding some green *zaatar* and a large round sesame bagel in a piece of ripped-up newspaper. I tore a piece of the warm bagel, dipped it into the savory-smelling *zaatar*, and took a bite.

Down below in the plaza, I saw a sea of black suits swaying in front of the only remaining wall of the Second Temple.[52] The devoted men below made me think of my first composition teacher, the one who taught me the art of writing symphonic scores. He was the master who led me into the hidden realm of sound, sharing with me the secrets behind the musical notes

---

52 The "Wailing Wall" is the major worship site for people of the Jewish faith. In Hebrew, it is called *Hakotel Hamaaravi* (literally, "Western Wall"), and it is believed to be the exterior western wall of the Second Temple, built by the Israelites in 538 B.C.E. and destroyed by the Romans in 70 C.E.

and opening the door into a world of ancient musical modes. He could have been down there among those people in black, who were praying and swaying in ecstasy.

My teacher was once one of the shining lights of the contemporary music world, which bestowed upon him, at a very early age, a prestigious teaching position at the Rubin Music Academy. I used to drive weekly to his humble home to take lessons, delving into the musical worlds of the ancient Near Eastern civilizations and the early-day European monasteries. I was only nineteen years old, but the master was already married with children. With his long black beard and feverish eyes, he impressed upon me the importance of maintaining control over the mood of each musical segment, applying the variety of musical modes the ancient Greeks used in their theatrical productions and rituals. He walked me through each mode, revealing its secrets, unique colors, and emotional tilts. It became clear to me then how each and every note has a special character and unique impact on the nature of the mode – and the mood of each given musical passage.

Then, my teacher disappeared.

Months earlier I had noticed that he was becoming increasingly fascinated by the mystical Jewish-Kabbalistic teachings and the daily practices of that path. Soon thereafter, he withdrew from public life, from the academy, and from composing and teaching the art of music. Then he vanished into the black sea of swaying suits near the one remaining holy wall in Jerusalem.

With relentless curiosity, I kept on studying the fascinating world of musical modes and moods, which originated in the East, moved to the West, and then faded away from Western culture. Most people are unaware of just how many musical modes have vanished from the West over the last thousand years. The Europeans inherited numerous forms of Eastern wisdom through the Greek, Arab and Persian civilizations, and this Eastern knowledge formed the foundation for much of the science and art that the Europeans developed over the last thousand years. But with regard to musical modes, the West has lost all but two modes: the Major, which in the West is considered "happy" or "bright," and the Minor, which Westerners typically describe as "sad" or "dark." The impact of this loss has had wide implications on Western civilization – culturally, psychologically, and neurologically – that are quite impossible to measure.

Consequently, recovering the vanishing modes is *vital,* because such a process would help Western civilization regain the full spectrum of emotional human expression. As writer Milan Kundera hinted in his book *The Unbearable Lightness of Being,* once we lose a way to express a human emotion, the capacity to actually feel that emotion may eventually fade away as well. For people in the West, regaining the vanishing modes might revive a bygone ability to feel and communicate certain complex emotions. For composers and musicians, the long-lost modes would provide a promise of a whole new universe of creative expression! However, such a potential, spectacular recovery depends on exploring and understanding the past, specifically the musical heritage of the East, which was entrusted to Western civilization hundreds of years ago.

"Without old, there is no new," states an old Middle Eastern proverb. Indeed, some European composers followed this sound wisdom. In the early 20th Century, the brilliant Russian composer Igor Stravinsky used melodies and rhythms of old, traditional Russian folk songs in revolutionary works that changed music for the concert hall and ballet and inspired millions of composers.[53] The great Hungarian composer Bella Bartok researched old gypsy folk songs of his homeland in order to create new and

---

53 Igor Stravinsky composed three symphonic masterpieces for the ballet: *The Rite of Spring, Firebird,* and *Petrushka.*

exciting music for the concert stage.[54] And when the 20th Century Estonian composer Arvo Part reached a dead end with his dissonant, contemporary-sounding symphonies, he resorted to a lengthy study of early musical forms from the Middle Ages. Part's historical studies resulted in his reemerging with a completely different musical style that promptly granted him tremendous acclaim and well-deserved worldwide recognition.[55]

Yet, in spite of all the creative output of the European composers over the last millennium, Western culture has essentially ignored the modes that were gifted to Europe by the Greeks, Romans, and Moors. Before vanishing during the second millennium, these modes still were part of the cultural fabric of Europe. It is well established that the Gregorian chants which the Catholic Church codified in the 6th Century were composed using ancient Near Eastern Greek modes.[56]

Thus, early European monks carried with them the heritage of contemplative and expressive modes that connected them *emotionally* and *culturally* to the Holy Land, the birthplace of their faith. However, people living in the West during the last thousand years likely have heard only the *Ionian* mode or Major scale as it is called in the West (i.e., the mode associated with "happiness"), and the *Aeolian* mode or Minor scale (associated

---

54 Bella Bartok is renowned for his symphonic masterpiece *Concerto for Orchestra*.

55 Arvo Part's masterpieces include *Cantus in Memoriam Benjamin Britten* (for string orchestra and bell) and *Fratres* (for cello ensemble).

56 The Gregorian chants sung by monks in Catholic monasteries were written using Greek modes, originally received from the Egyptians and Babylonians. But European scholars misread the Greek manuscripts, misnamed individual modes, and referred to them collectively as the "Church Modes." Nevertheless, the notes of each mode match those of ancient Greece. The modes are: *Ionian* (same musical notes as Major scale CDEFGAB); *Dorian* (DEFGABC); *Phrygian* (EFGABCD); *Lydian* (FGABCDE); *Mixolydian* (GABCDF); *Aeolian* (same notes as Minor scale ABCDEFG); and *Lucian* or *Locrian* (BCDEFGA).

in the West with "sadness"). Moreover, regardless of whether classical, folk, pop, rock, jazz or any other contemporary musical style is being played, almost all the music composed in Europe and the Americas for the past thousand years has been created using only two musical modes!

Isn't it astonishing that all the wonderful classical repertoire composed by the great masters such as Bach, Beethoven and Mozart and nearly all the dance, folk, and pop songs ever recorded in the West have been created using just the Major and Minor modes?[57]

In the context of painting, it would be like being doomed to use only black and white colors! Indeed, wonderful master-pieces can be created using only the gray scale (the spectrum between black and white). Still, that two-tone palette would significantly limit the range of an artist's expression, compared to the full-color spectrum we see in nature all around us.

---

57 There are a few exceptions. Some Celtic folk songs and pop songs, such as Paul Simon's "Scarborough Fair," utilize the *Dorian* mode. Handfuls of pop songs are written in *Mixolydian* mode, such as "Norwegian Wood" by the Beatles. And there are modal jazz compositions, such as Miles Davis' "So What" composed in *Dorian* mode, that use modal phrasings within the theme. Typically, however, jazz improvisations that follow these themes betray the modal characteristics and fall back on common jazz and blues phrasing. Within the concert stage world, the modes have been seldom used, with the exception of the great European masters, such as Bela Bartok and Gabriel Faure, who each composed a work by the same title of "Lydia," written in the ancient *Lydian* mode.

Other exceptions can be found among small and traditionally isolated ethnic groups, such as Jews and Gypsies, who kept using the Near Eastern musical modes of their ancestors despite being assimilated in the West. For example, the East European Jewish Klezmer modes and the Central European Jewish cantorial chanting modes are directly related to the Middle Eastern modes, as is the cantorial mode Ahava Raba, which is the same as the Near Eastern mode *makam Hijaz* (i.e., both modes use the musical notes EFG#ABCD).

Contrary to the West, in the East today, as in ancient days, the musical modes have been providing composers, clergy, and communities a variety of modes that are capable of evoking and expressing a wide range of nuanced and complex psychological moods. Just like native plants, these musical modes are the fruit of the land, and their essence stems from the unique geography of their original terrain. This system of expressive moods and nuanced emotions is like having a whole world of color, an ocean of musical currents!

In Arabic, this system of modes is called *makamat*, which is the plural form of the word *makam*, or *makom* in Hebrew, which means a "station," "place," or "phase." In the West, a music teacher would tell students, "Today we are going to learn the C Major scale," which implies moving up and down the scale, thereby preparing the children's minds to regard music as technology and the musical scale as a mechanical or technological tool. Similarly in the Netherlands, the concept of musical scale is called a "tonal ladder." By comparison, the Eastern term *makam* would lead a teacher to tell students: "Today we will learn *makam Hijaz*," literally the "place of Hijaz." Thus, the musical scale is not regarded as a mechanical tool in the East. Rather it is viewed as a place. What kind of place? It is an *emotional* place! Accordingly, each and every mode is a domain with which we may express a unique psychological phase or state of mind.[58]

And so this entire system of Near Eastern modes has been used by Jews, Christians, and Muslims of the Middle East to create sacred and folk music for different purposes.

---

58 This designation of the *makamat* as a system of "emotional places" also is evident in the name *modus,* which the Romans gave to the Greek musical scales (i.e., "modes" relate to "moods").

Accordingly, some *makamat* have been employed in festive celebrations; others, in rituals and ceremonies. Additionally, special modes have been used for holidays, such as Yom Kippur ("Day of Atonement" in the Jewish tradition), while other modes have been utilized for circumcision rituals, weddings, joyful parties, and songs of praise. Even more fascinating is the fact that the various ethnic groups and opposing religious groups of the Middle East have been using these modes to express similar emotions via similar modes!

This realization led me to suspect that the musical modes predate religious and ethnic divides and represent a natural outcome of the unique environment of the region, just as unique as its native vegetation. The sound of the wind blowing through the desert canyons of the Middle East is different than any sound I have ever heard on the other continents. The feeling of these desolate lands – the yellow desert sand, the warm blue sea that meets the yellow dunes, and the crisp mountain air which one poet described as "transparent as wine with the aroma of pine trees"[59] – are as distinctive as their musical modes.

Nowadays, the contemporary music of the Middle East and the Far East exhibit strong Western influence, rejecting all of the modes except two: the Major and the Minor. Unless you listen to traditional folk or sacred music from the East, you would think that all other modes had vanished from the Earth. And it is not only the musical modes that have been vanishing. Various sounds have been disappearing from contemporary languages as well.

---

59 From the poem "Jerusalem of Gold," by Naomi Shemer.

Currently, spoken Hebrew is missing some of the ancient accents, pronunciations that survive only among one ethnic group of Yemenite Jews.[60] In addition, present-day French is missing sounding consonants that it had in the past, and contemporary English no longer includes some of the sound expressions that have survived only as silent consonants, such as the "k" sound in the word "know."

As far as sound vibrations and emotional ranges go, human expressions via music and language have been shrinking. As the rate of change in our daily lives has greatly accelerated over the last thousand years, we have unwittingly reduced and narrowed the spectrum of sound and emotional expression for communication and the creation of art. We have left behind the treasures of nuanced sound and language at a crucial time in our evolutionary journey, at the very moment that the natural environment is crying out to us for consideration and mercy.

That day, while I stood in Jerusalem overlooking the Wailing Wall, I saw people kissing the sacred stones, some praying aloud with a book, others dancing in joyful, ecstatic circles. I saw men swaying in quiet meditation, some pleading to God, while others shed tears of pain. I noticed grown-ups acting like children and complete strangers sharing instant intimacy. Near that old stone wall – an ancient symbol of the Divine – I witnessed human expression that transcended individual consciousness, a vast spectrum of devotion which revealed our potential power and our collective promise of Oneness ...

---

60 Examples are the sound of the third letter of the Hebrew alphabet *gimel* (*dagesh* accent), and the sound of the fourth letter *daled* (*dagesh* accent).

And for a split second, I thought I heard the voice of my music composition teacher rhetorically exclaim:

Imagine the prospect for intricate, colorful music and the renaissance of interpersonal communication that the Western world could experience if only the songwriters of today would compose again with the endless treasures of the vanishing modes.[61]

---

61 To hear original music composed by Yuval Ron using these modes, listen to these tracks: "Opening Titles" from the CD *West Bank Story*, written in *makam Kurd*, which is the same as the *Phrygian* church mode (www.cduniverse.com/productinfo.asp?pid=7431662&style=music); "Messina" from the CD *Proteus: A 19th Century Vision*, written in *Dorian* mode (www.cdbaby.com/cd/yuval6); "Sim Shalom" from the CD *Oud Prayers on the Road to St. Jacques*, written in *makam Hijaz* (www.cdbaby.com/cd/yuval8); "Kholat Ahava" from the CD *Tree of Life*, written in *makam Kurd* (www.cdbaby.com/cd/yuval5); "Taqsim in A Hijaz" from the CD *Rilke: Searching for the Inner Soul*, written in *makam Hijaz* (www.cdbaby.com/cd/ronwaldman).

CHAPTER XI

The Story of the Oud

This is one of the most fascinating stories in the world of music. Yet, it is more than a story. It is a sliver of human history that has vanished from public knowledge in the Western world for more than one thousand years! Nonetheless, it has impacted everyone who has ever picked up the guitar, and it has left a permanent mark on the heritage of Spain, the music of the European troubadours, and the music of the Middle East and North Africa. And all this came about because one master teacher failed the ultimate test ...

It all started in Baghdad, the grand city on the bank of the two great rivers of Babylon, which sits on the Silk Road which led from Italy to China. Every perfume, every spice, every precious silk, and every other good went through that city for hundreds of years.

The proud ruler of this metropolis – the Khalif – became the richest and most powerful king of the ancient world during the 8ᵗʰ Century. And he had an insatiable appetite for all exquisite things. The best artists in the world lived in his court, the finest chefs cooked in his kitchens, the top musicians and dancers entertained him each evening, and the smartest scholars and scientists studied endlessly in his enormous libraries. The Khaif was so proud of his archives and his collections of new Arabic translations of the great treasures of ancient Greece that he called it *Beit El Khokhma* (the "House of Wisdom").

No doubt, the Khalif also wished to possess the best oud player in the entire world. So from Musul, a faraway city in the north, he elicited *the* world master of that very ancient four-stringed instrument – an old man named Ishak Al Musuli.

Each night, Master Ishak would entertain the Khalif with meditative, dark sounds that poured out of the ornate and ancient lute of the East. And soon the Khalif, who was a music student himself, was humming along with each note of Master Ishak's tunes.

One day in the middle of his afternoon nap, The Khalif of Baghdad heard a knock at his chamber door. *Who is knocking?* he thought. *It must be my spy!* (As you well know, every king needs a spy who listens to what is going on behind the king's back!)

The spy came in and said in a soft voice, "Honorable Khalif, you have enjoyed the recitals of Master Ishak for a long time now, believing that he is the greatest master of the oud, the best oud player in the entire empire. I hereby inform you that you have been misled! There is a secret – a secret that old snake has been keeping from you all this time."

"A musical secret?" laughed the Khalif, greatly entertained by the idea that his court master musician could hide anything at all from him.

"Yes, indeed," whispered the spy. "It is a musical secret and Master Ishak has kept it from you! One of his students, a young black man, is in my humble opinion the greatest living oud player in this entire blessed world!"

The Khalif was very disturbed. How could it be? Both the Khalif and the spy were music students of the old master. They knew the oud, and they loved its deep, dark, meditative tone, its crying voice, and its beautiful inlaid wooden belly.

"Go!" roared the Khalif. "Let the court know that I have now ordered a special solo oud recital featuring that black man immediately after dinner tonight. Tell me, what is his name, what is the musician's name?"

"Ziryab," yelled the spy as he ran out of the chamber. "We call him 'Ziryab the Black Bird.' "

Before too long, Master Ishak was summoned before the Khalif. "I have recently heard there may be a most talented oud student who you haven't had a chance yet to present to me," said the Khalif with a calm, intonated voice.

"You mean … Ziryab, most honorable Khalif?" Master Ishak trembled in front of his king and his voice turned to a raspy whisper, "But he is not one of us! He is a black man from Africa, or from Persia …. Forget about him, honorable Khalif, that Ziryab is a strange man!"

The Khalif's face morphed into an artificial smile, as he became more and more curious. He turned to his aide and ordered him to reschedule the recital at once, *before* dinner. "And make sure you are there, Master Ishak. I want *you* at the recital this evening!" ordered the Khalif in a deep voice that bellowed throughout the entire palace. The guards grabbed Master Ishak and removed him from the King's presence.

The sun was heading toward the faraway holy city of the west, as the Khalif waited impatiently on his throne. Then, the door to the grand hall opened. Ziryab, a tall and handsome dark-skinned man walked in. He was the noblest man the Khalif had ever seen, but he had no instrument with him. The Khalif looked at the guards. The guards seemed a bit nervous. *What is this man scheming?* they thought. *He arrives to play a concert for the Khalif without his instrument!*

"Come close my son," said the Kaliph. "Here is my oud. Come and play your beautiful melodies on my precious instrument." Then the Khalif lifted his oud toward Ziryab.

But the young student signaled with a slow hand motion that he was rejecting the offer. The guards were stunned. Their blood pressure shot a few notches higher. How could this man refuse the will of the great Khalif of Baghdad?

Yet Ziryab surprised everyone, as he opened his mouth and said with an intonated, high-pitched voice, "Grand Khalif, if you wish me to play the old songs you know by heart – the compositions of my teacher, Master Ishak – then I will play them on your precious oud. However, if you would rather hear the melodies of the future, tunes you have never heard before … well then, for that, I will have to fetch my own special oud, which I built myself and presently left behind at the entrance hall."

Now, the Khalif turned even more suspicious, as all the guards began to sweat. But more than that, the Khalif was intrigued by the notion that Zriyab might play new melodies on his special oud, tunes that the king had never heard. "Bring in the case, the case with his oud!" ordered the Khalif with a dry and biting tone. The guards immediately brought in the oud case.

Slowly and calmly, Ziryab took out the oud. It seemed just like all other ouds, but upon a closer look, Ziryab's oud had an extra string! "You see Grand Khalif, I have added a bass string made of lion gut. I removed it from the belly of a lion that I caught with my own bare hands."

Master Ishak nearly exploded with rage, "What have you done? You added a string! How dare you ruin our ancient noble instrument!"

Ziryab remained as cool as a fish, "I prefer the sound of five strings. I like to have more bass for *my* oud."

The Khalif had no patience left in him. "Stop this nonsensical chatter – *yallah, yallah, yallah.* Start playing, and no more talking in this chamber right now!"

Ziryab sat down, closed his eyes, waited for several long seconds and then began to play. At once, the birds outside the windows turned silent. Ziryab's long, tanned fingers danced over the strings, performing effortless feats of musical magic.

The Khalif's soul went straight to the seventh heaven! He had never heard such an intricate and beautiful melody before and with such a complicated rhythmic pattern. And the sound: The tone of that oud was deep and dark, like the color of the best olive oil the court used to get from northern mountain villages. Ziryab's oud had a hypnotic and seductive voice, like no other oud in the world.

Throughout the night, that oud's voice continued to sing in each of the Khalif's dreams. The next morning, the Khalif was awakened up by loud knocks on his chamber doors. *Who is knocking?* he wondered. *Could it be my spy again?*

It was the spy. "I am here to report, most honorable Khalif, that with great effort and skill I have uncovered a terrible scheme to harm …"

The Khalif, who was accustomed to being the target of occasional schemes, cut the spy off in a sleepy but determined voice, "Who is plotting to kill me this time? Go on, tell me the name of the traitor, and I will see to it that his head is chopped off by lunch time today."

"I regret to notify you, grand Khalif, that this time the scheme does not concern *you!* It is about …" continued the spy, now whispering, "a man who, in my humble view, is the greatest oud master alive. It is a plot to harm Ziryab!"

Across town, at the very same time, there was a nervous knock at the door to Ziryab's house. *Who is knocking?* wondered Ziryab.

The door opened with shrieking sounds. Master Ishak, pale like a half moon, stood at the threshold. "You have two choices, Ziryab," he said with a low raspy voice. "You may stay here, but I will in turn make your life miserable. I will ruin you, your family, your career and your entire life!" His voice then morphed into a sharp whisper. "Or, you may leave Baghdad, disappear with your children, your wives, and your five-stringed oud. Move far away, to the very end of the great earth, and I will pay for all your expenses!"

The two great musicians faced each other. It was the crucial moment: when a teacher faces the ultimate test – the point at which a student is capable of surpassing the master's abilities. For an educator, it is *the* moment of truth. And Master Ishak failed this test miserably.

Ziryab was a man of imagination, a creator of art and beauty. He disliked conflict, and so he decided to leave Baghdad. He took his oud and went where his master told him to go – to the end of the world.

Neither man was aware that this also was an historic moment. Master Ishak's failure ultimately would lead Ziryab to change the musical and cultural history of faraway continents. As a consequence of his student's fall from grace, the old master unknowingly pushed him to travel to Europe and alter the cultural development of the western world.

The young Ziryab walked west, because he knew that Spain (or Al-Andalus as the Arabs called it then) was as far as one could walk until reaching the end of the earth and the beginning of the infinite waters. He walked through Egypt and North Africa. He walked with his family all the way to Morocco, and then he crossed the narrow waters between Africa and Europe, finally arriving in the court of Cordoba, the provincial capital of Al-Andalus (southern Spain today).

The "New World" was waiting beyond the great, great sea. Yet at that time, no one could have known that there was land beyond Al-Andalus. And at this provincial place, young Ziryab – the brilliant musical pioneer – became the court composer of Cordoba, the city that would eventually become the cultural center of the Islamic Empire and the most sophisticated place on earth in the fields of science and art.

By the end of his life, Ziryab had revolutionized the music of Andalusia. In Cordoba, he opened the first music conservatory in Europe, where he taught Spanish youth how to play the oud (which they mistakenly called "lute," mispronouncing the Arabic *el-oud*). He and his fellow Muslims brought a total of twenty-three new instruments to Europe and a whole system of Middle Eastern musical modes (the *makamat*), and they laid the foundation for the Andalusi style of music, which was a predecessor of flamenco, a style of music later created by the gypsies in the same lands.

The European lute, which featured more strings and frets, was developed from Ziryab's oud. The Europeans also developed the Baroque and Renaissance lutes and, later on, the classical guitar. Thanks to Ziryab, later-day troubadours used these instruments to play the musical modes brought to Europe by the Moors, dark-skinned countrymen of Ziryab.

These indigenous Middle Eastern musical modes also impacted the church music and folk songs of Spain. From then on, Spanish music would deviate from other European music, just as Spanish architecture and cuisine would never be the same.

Thus, Ziryab was an influential pioneer not only in music but also in fashion, hair styling, cuisine and commerce. He and his wife became role models of the rapidly developing high society of Cordoba. Everyone sought an invite to Ziryab's house for a meal, and everyone wanted to emulate his hairstyle, his manners, his way of dress and, of course, his intricate and stellar music. In addition, Ziryab explored spirituality through his music. He had the oud strings marked in different symbolic colors to correspond with the ancient elements of nature: earth, air, fire, water, and spirit.

Truly, Ziryab's impact on Andalusia was extraordinary, but the Europeans have rarely shared his story. They have neglected to mention Ziryab's influence on the western world because he was a Middle Eastern man and an icon of a Muslim civilization, a highly sophisticated population which would be purged from Spain within a few centuries.[62]

Yet in the collective Arabic memory, Ziryab's legacy as a great composer and music theoretician was never lost. "The Nubas," which are musical suites he composed in Spain, form the foundation of nearly all of the classical music of North Africa and the Middle East. Indeed, the young oud student who was exiled to the end of the known world ended up being the "Johann Sebastian Bach" of the classical Arabic music world.

Thus, despite the fact that for the last thousand years Spanish history books have failed to mention the true story of the oud, history now is recalling Ziryab. Thankfully, what started as a dark and petty moment – when a jealous master teacher failed the ultimate test – now ends as a luminous legacy.[63]

---

62 The first western scholar to break the taboo and bring Ziryab back to life was Julian Ribera, a Spanish linguist, who in 1922, courageously published the book *La Musica de las Cantigas*, dedicated to the influence of Arabic musicians on Spanish music and culture. Yet to this day, the story of the oud and the history of Ziryab are not being taught by the great majority of music schools in the West.

63 You may listen to a tribute by the legendary Spanish master flamenco musician Paco de Lucia, which he dedicated to Ziryab, on his 1992 CD entitled *Zyryab*.

CHAPTER XII

The Mystery of Unplanned Creativity

The great jazz pianist Keith Jarrett was improvising. His muffled, raspy voice was doubling the sounds of the piano, as his fingers ran up and down the ebony and ivory keys. He was making it up on the spot, and the result was a brilliant flow of several hundred musical notes per minute!

The flood of notes was so swift, unplanned and yet so perfectly musical, one has to wonder: *What lies behind that phenomenal expression of human creativity? Who was choosing the notes? Was it Keith Jarrett? Could it have been an autonomous musical center within his brain? Or maybe it was a Supreme Power above and beyond the master jazz pianist?* This is one of the greatest mysteries of human nature and the creative life.

Growing up, I was an avid reader of memoirs and biographies of master musicians, dancers, writers, artists, and inventors. There was an air of adventure in these historical chronicles of human creativity, which always fascinated me. I sensed there was something magical in the creative process, something no one fully understood.

That mystery invited much contemplation by the scientists of the inner realm – the mystics of the East – who provided us with fascinating and inspiring insights into the nature of creation and creativity, human and divine. Early on, I began seeking some of these sources of inspiration, which led me to a continuous exploration of the deep ocean of mystical Kabbalah and Sufi teachings.[64]

Now, when I explore a free-form musical improvisation, I attempt to create without any framework. At the very outset, I have no preference for any musical mode, scale, theory, rhythmic patterns, images, or themes. My only references are the space I am in, the living beings around me, and my own self, and by that I mean the inner voice I may hear coming through me. These three types of references or vibrations are the only guides for the musical journey I take. It is a form of meditation, an exploration, and a sense of delightful adventure, during which I discover unplanned sounds and emotional expressions.

When I reach the conclusion of such improvisation, I am often without words, savoring and holding on to that blessed silence and sacred stillness to which I have arrived. All the musical notes that I improvise on the way to that silence are merely corridors, paths, or necessary ladders to deeper and higher places. I often realize that I play some musical elements that I have never ever played before, note combinations and human expressions I never learned from a teacher or heard from other musicians. Sometimes, I get to explore sounds that I normally would consider errors, such as squeaking sounds. I don't know why I play such squeaky or muffled notes, but that's what comes to me, that's what inserts itself into the flow, and I don't know from where it originates.

---

64 For example, one of the Kabbalistic concepts involves the "four worlds," which represent four different qualities of creativity.

This mystery points to an energetic source which is beyond music and art. It is always there behind the scene and may affect the way we might ride a horse, ride a bike, sail a boat, or make love. It is hiding below the surface when we dance, when we play sports, when we garden, and even when we simply talk. Yes, the "art of life" means to consciously and subconsciously collaborate with that flow of mysterious energy, to sense its direction, and to ride it, flow with it ... *or* let it ride us.

To understand the mechanism behind this hidden potential energy, neuroscientists scan the brains of improvising musicians who are masters of the art of unplanned creativity. One researcher recruited several jazz pianists and placed them, one at the time, in an MRI machine, which uses powerful magnets and sound waves to create a scan of the inner organs of the human body.[65] The pianists had to memorize a pre-composed blues tune and then perform it on a small electronic musical keyboard that rested on their laps, while lying on their backs inside the MRI machine. Their brains were scanned to the maximum possible detail. Then, they were told to simply improvise a tune based on the general format of a blues song – an unplanned musical improvisation over a twelve-bar blues accompaniment.

The MRI machine scanned their brains during these improvisations and provided an amazing view of the inside of the musicians' brains. The scans revealed that while improvising, an area of the artist's brain that involves autobiographical memory and self-expression becomes very active. This region of the brain is not nearly as active when a pianist performs memorized, pre-composed, or non-improvised pieces. Moreover, a different area of the brain associated with self-criticizing, judging, sizing and measuring went to sleep while the pianists were improvising.

---

65 Charles Limb, M.D., Associate Professor of Otolaryngology and Head and Neck Surgery at John Hopkins University.

How fascinating! When we truly improvise – in any arena – we let go of judgment and we let ourselves create without quality control. The possibility of emotion-directed, subconscious memories rises to awareness during this state of mind, allowing us to express something personal and unique, like autobiographical stories which unveil our deep inner selves, our birth experience, long-forgotten events that happened in our childhoods, or possibly even remnants we carry with us from the "collective consciousness." These profound personal impressions come through us when we create without judgment.

I believe this state of mind is not exclusive to improvisational music and may occur when a great master pianist performs a pre-composed piece (such as a Mozart concerto) and the performance is done in an ecstatic state, a condition where the pianist forgets all about the memorized notes, forgets the self, and lets go of judgment. The pianist's fingers then hit the right keys on the piano because of muscle memory formed during numerous hours of practicing and memorizing that piece of music. But the mind of the pianist is not conscious of that information; instead, he allows an uncontrolled flow of creativity to channel through him. The pianist is then able to play the Mozart piece as if he were improvising it on the spot, without controlling or judging it, with freshness and vitality in every note, as if the pianist were playing it for the very first time. During such performances of truly high art, some feel the presence of a sacred and elusive bliss. The visit of that grace stems from the performer's ability to give up some control and leave a space for an appearance of the unruly "Queen of Wisdom," whom the ancient Near East mystics called Sophia.

The European painters and poets of the 18th and 19th Centuries called her the "muse."[66] One day, there might be a wonderful

---

66 Originally from Greek mythology, the Muses were the goddesses of inspiration in the fields of art and science. The word "muse" also is the source of the Greek word *mousikê* and the Latin word *musica* (music).

flow of creativity thanks to the visit of the muse, yet the next day might yield lousy work, all because the muse didn't show up. By crediting or blaming a metaphysical goddess, artists (including the atheists among them) clearly acknowledged that there was something greater beyond themselves that was profoundly affecting the process of their creativity.

Yuval Ron with a "Muse" in an inspired performance

When a critic writes in a concert review, "It was an inspired performance" or "the solo pianist, the conductor, and the entire orchestra were inspired tonight and crafted a magnificent performance," that critic is describing a mystical experience.

The readers may not notice, but the critic is informing them that there was "spirit" inside the artists and thanks to that spirit, the performance was magical. "Inspire" literally means a "spirit inside" or "inhaling breath or wind." In mystical terminology, "breath" and "wind" (from the Hebrew word *ruach*) mean the Breath of Life, in other words, the Creator.

Human beings have referred to this life force and its various attributes by many terms, yet none truly captures its complete nature. We may call it Breath of Life, God, Muse, Spirit, The Tao, Bliss, Grace, Self, Wise Self, Atman, and so forth. We may feel its presence better than we can describe it. What we do know is that it is beyond our control, and so the creative process is ultimately a collaboration between us and this intangible, elusive energy.

Once we admit that we do not fully control the situation, we allow ourselves to feel vulnerable. Performing artists and writers often admit such vulnerability when they acknowledge that in spite of making every effort to prepare, the merit of their creative output always varies. Even if they try to make an exact science out of their preparations, schedule, diet, location and conditions, the quality of their work still will shift and vary. This vulnerability – which is inherent in the creative process – has led many artists into spiritual explorations.

The great jazz saxophonist John Coltrane was one such seeker. He explored Christianity, Buddhism, mystical Kabbalistic Jewish teaching, and Islam. In the end, he arrived at something he called "Universalism" or "Universal Love," which he expressed in his well-known composition entitled, "A Love Supreme." Yet, his search did not clarify the mysterious unfolding of the creative process.

Back in the 13th Century, Rumi, the mystic Sufi poet, gave us an inspiring insight into this mystery. He saw the reed flute, the ney, as a metaphor for the human being. By observing the process of making the ney, Rumi noted that the flute maker would go to the riverbank and cut a reed from its birthplace, separating it from its origins. Then, the flute maker would roast the reed in fire to make it stronger and afterward drill seven holes through it.

Now imagine blowing through that reed: independent from its birthplace, free of its upbringing, strengthened by the fire, and carrying the pain of the holes. *What kind of sound do you think would it produce?*

Even if you were a great master flutist, you would not get any sound out of that reed because it is not hollow. True, the flute maker drilled seven holes through it, but it's still full and needs to be hollowed out. It needs to be empty! Only then is the breath able to go through it and produce a sound.

Every artist and every human being is a flute, an instrument, a vessel, or a conduit. In order to make a sound, in order to create, we need to be empty first. That is the reason for the moments of silence that precede many musical performances.

In the Hindu tradition, a musician does three different tunings before he strikes a note. First, the musical instrument has to be tuned. Then, the musician sits still and tunes himself. In other words, he attempts to become empty by clearing his mind from all images and thoughts. Sometimes this stage of attunement also includes making an inner dedication or invocation. Lastly, the musician performs one more tuning. He attempts to tune the audience. With his mind, the master musician reaches out to the hearts of audience members, attuning and stilling them, until they are as tuned as the musical instrument and the mind of the musician. Only then can the first note be struck and the concert be commenced.

Some may think this practice of tuning the audience is a delusion or unscientific, mystical assumption. Yet, contemporary neuroscientists are now studying the phenomenon of manipulating the brain of another, which has led to the discovery of special brain cells called mirror neurons.[67]

Therefore, when it is time to create or to improvise, you should begin with a period of attunement. This is relevant to any task, not only to what we conventionally consider artistic activities, since every act in life should be approached as an art. Every teacher, butcher, athlete, surgeon, and truck driver would benefit from such attunement at the outset of each workday. If a majority of us would perform such a practice, imagine how we might transform our world!

Just remember the results of the research done by neuroscientists on jazz pianists: In the initial stage of creativity when the spark of wisdom is called upon, criticizing, judging, and self-awareness should be stifled. The capacity for expressing some sort of conscious or unconscious personal story should be activated. This is when you may become a channel for inspiration, for wisdom of your true nature, for your inner divine voice to sing through you. At this stage, there are no rules or framework, just a flow. Later on, you may develop, shape, edit and finalize the creation, using your judgmental and intellectual capabilities. In sum, the practice of unplanned creativity is an opportunity for all of us – not only artists and scientists – to find new ground, new ideas, and learn more about the true depth of the universe around and inside of ourselves.

If you wish to create, I suggest that you dedicate a special time for such exploration, possibly once a week, once a month, or once a day and devote ten to twenty minutes of attunement and improvisation, exploring something new that may come out of you. You may express this spark of creativity through writing, talking, drawing, moving, playing, singing, or thinking. No matter what you do, you are better off letting it flow though you in collaboration with the mystery of the depths, rather than

---

67 See the work of neuroscientist Vilayanur Ramachandran, Ph.D.

controlling and judging what you are producing. Such a practice will enrich and inform your life as much as working with and being aware of your dreams.

In the future, I expect that science will have more sophisticated tools to track and further explain the process of human creativity and the collaboration between human beings and the great flow of energy, which we call "inspiration." However, I doubt that science will ever demystify this mysterious force which, upon the surrender of critical control, might blow a divine sound through us.

The great master musicians Keith Jarrett and John Coltrane did not wait for any scientific explanations. They let Sophia flow through them and, as co-creating partners, went on a spectacular musical ride. You can do it too, in life and in art!

CHAPTER XIII

Art Out of Darkness

One day, one thousand years ago, a tribe of master musicians and dancers of the court of the King of Rajasthan started to walk westbound, following the sun. And nobody knows, nobody is certain, why they left the court. They just walked and walked for five hundred years until they reached the end of the earth – a place where, if they had kept walking west, they would have simply walked into the great blue sea and drowned.

This was the end of the earth, a place the Arabs called Al-Andalus. And when these master musicians and dancers – whom we incorrectly call Gypsies – finally arrived at the southern tip of Andalusia, they heard the centuries-old Arab-Jewish Andalusi music: old soulful music that was brought by the Arabs and the Jews who wandered off to Andalusia, Spain from the faraway Middle East many centuries past. That music, which was cooked and boiled for generations in the hot bountiful lands of Andalusia, was now ready to receive a new twist, a new spellbound re-write by the newcomer chefs from Rajasthan – the Gypsies, or as they would rather be called, the Roma people.

Yet, the sunny fields of Andalusia would not be the place where the Roma people unveiled their brilliant contribution to human culture. The open, yellow wheat fields and the green olive tree orchards – as inviting and alluring as they were – would not be the place where Flamenco would be born. Rather, in their new home called Al-Andalus, the Gypsy families had little choice but to stay in the dark, cool caves hidden in the mountainsides. These chains of white cavities in the belly of the mountains stayed cool in the burning summer heat and stayed warm in the bone-chilling winters. More than anything, the caves protected the Gypsies from the Spaniards, from persecution, and from death.

Within these stone cave walls, the master musicians and dancers of a lost paradise kept the old, complex rhythms alive. Eventually, the ornamental melodies of the Arab and Jewish people of Al-Andalus began to find their way into the accented Romani beats of old India. And a marriage was made on a fiery day in heaven: East met the Middle East in the fertile red lands of the hot and bloody Iberian Peninsula.

One of the Gypsy families that made these caves their home had a young, beautiful, and sweet girl named Carmen. That precious young girl had big, black, fiery eyes and long black hair. Her hair bounced off her back as she danced. And she loved to dance and she loved to sing, but more than *anything*, she loved her father, her Papa. However, she was never allowed to dance and sing out in the sunny meadows. She had to stay inside the damp, dark cave in the mountainside, just across the canyon from the enormous Alhambra castle, where the Spanish elite would leisurely sip mint tea and pomegranate juice in their lush, exquisite gardens.

One day, Carmen approached her father, as she was frustrated with their kind of life. She complained to him about the darkness of the cave, about being confined to the Andalusian mountainside. Papa listened and hugged her with *all* that he had in him. Then he said with an increasingly ecstatic voice, "Listen to Papa,

Carmen. One day, you and your children will create something out of this darkness. You will create something *incredible*. You will create music and dance. You will create art and beauty. Like the lotus flower that comes out of the mud, like our brothers and sisters the African slaves who will one day create a grand form of art out of their suffering, you Carmen, *you* will create something out of this darkness! You will birth music and dance that will become the *soul* of Spain!

"One day, many years from now, people will come to the finest place in the capital, Madrid, to hear this music and watch such dance. People will *pay* to see it, even people from the government will stand in line to buy a ticket to see your children and your grandchildren perform the national music and dance of Spain. And art museums around the *whole* world will present that music and dance so their audiences can be inspired and stunned. They will consider it to be the highest art of Spain, the *soul* of Spain! You will see Carmen, you will see. Listen to Papa."

Hundreds of years later, a noble, complex and inspired art formed out of darkness. Flamenco is its name, and within it resides the promise that the human spirit – such a creative and adaptable life force – always will endure, adapt and outlive the cry that brought it forth.[68]

---

68 In 2010, I traveled to Andalusia, Spain, to create a new concert program with the gypsy musicians and dancers of Seville and Jerez. In 2011, I titled the program "Soul of Spain" and presented it at the World Festival of Sacred Music in Los Angeles (www.youtube.com/watch?v=qrOTlCG6O1o). National Public Radio described it as "an extraordinary testament to music's transforming power and inspirational reach. In a vivid program, the Yuval Ron Ensemble – with guest gypsy flamenco musicians and dancers – explores the Jewish and Gypsy traditions of Andalusia, Spain. With fiery Flamenco and Sephardic Jewish music, dance and fascinating storytelling, the Ensemble delves deep into the region's cultural heart and celebrates its beat."

The story of Carmen and her father came through me during that extraordinary production in Los Angeles. It is based on historical accounts and musicological research that inspired me throughout the "Soul of Spain" concerts and rehearsals.

CHAPTER XIV

Why Sound Is Important

I have been fascinated with sound from a very early age. I recall a time when I was in my parents' car at a gas station, listening to the clacking sound of the fuel hoses being pulled off and returned to the pumps. I couldn't help but notice that there was an interesting beat in those clacking sounds. An even earlier memory brings back to my ears a magical harmony I heard at a tender age, when my babysitter strummed the strings of her guitar.

I have studied sound throughout my adult life. During my training in film scoring at Berklee College of Music, I explored the psycho-acoustic effects of sound. Later on, I became interested in its use within various mystical traditions. In recent times, through my work with researchers of the human brain, I have studied the impact of sound on healing and well-being.

The power of sound is apparent in everyday life. You may have observed people who dislike cleaning a house or doing other physical work turn on some upbeat music in the background while they are working. Once the music is on, their lack of vitality evaporates and they immediately awaken and become energized. All of a sudden, they have the power to do their chores.

Rhythmic sound affects us on a motoric level. It's not just about listening to sound through our ears. We also hear sound waves as they vibrate though our skin, flesh, and bones. Scientists have confirmed that humans and animals spontaneously synchronize their motion to the rhythmic sounds they hear.[69] We see it mostly in children, who immediately dance when rhythmic music is played. As we age, however, a majority of us become stiff and resist acting upon spontaneous responses to music. We end up suppressing our innate tendency to move to rhythmic sound. Nevertheless, it must be stated that we can re-awaken the natural instinctive response between sound and bodily movement at any age.

We see the impact of sound on various other aspects of life as well. Some people spend the majority of their waking hours in "gray" offices, sitting next to "gray" computers, doing "gray" kinds of a jobs that they don't truly like. Often, the introduction of music into such a "monochrome" world saves peoples' lives. The harmonic nature of the musical sounds that enter a workspace through various electronic devices helps people survive the challenges of an otherwise dreary and possibly harmful environment.

Over the years, I have observed several accountants who would have left their line of work, had they not been permitted to play classical music in the background to make their work tolerable. Such "musical medicine" enables them to feel

69 See two research papers: "Experimental Evidence for Synchronization to a Musical Beat in a Nonhuman Animal," by A.D. Patel, Ph.D., et. al. of the Neurosciences Institute in San Diego, CA (2009), and "Joint Drumming: Social Context Facilitates Synchronization in Preschool Children," by Marc Kirschner, Ph.D., et. al. of the Max Planck Institute for Evolutionary Anthropology in Leipzig, Germany (2009).

comfortable and content at their offices. Thus, the presence of beauty and harmony can counter-balance a lack of nourishment in dismal workplaces.

Music is defined in Japanese as "pleasurable noise." I would define music as "harmonic sound," as this definition accurately implies that music is a complex structure of sound waves which exist in accord with one another (accord = chord = harmony). That "accordance" provides pleasure to humans and other living beings. Some of the mystical Sufi masters say that the "harmonic sound we hear tunes the human body and spirit, and like a master musician tuning a musical instrument, it improves the output (and the health) of the human being."[70] Various clinical studies of music therapy procedures are now confirming this ancient mystical knowledge.[71] As a result, what the ancient yogis called *Nada Yoga* (yoga of sound) is now becoming one of the best tools in the West for treating insomnia, anxiety, depression, and stress.

We rarely are aware of how deep and intimate the experience of sound actually is. When you hear the sound of a speaking voice, you most likely are not aware that the speaker's vocal cords are vibrating air. The air column comes out of the speaker's mouth, sending out a set of sound waves that travel through the air, then bounce off the floor, the ceiling and the walls. The nature of the space we are in determines how many reflections of the initial sound waves we actually will feel/hear in our bodies.

In a cathedral, for example, you may hear lots of reflections of the initial sound waves, and the resulting impact will be rich and complex. All these sound waves – all these vibrations of air – then travel into your ear and vibrate a piece of skin called the

---

70 See the book *Mysticism of Sound and Music*, by Hazrat Inayat Khan.

71 See the research paper entitled "A Neuroscientific Perspective on Music Therapy," by Stefan Koelsch, Ph.D., of the University of Sussex, Falmer, Brighton, United Kingdom (2009). Dr. Koelsch's findings indicated that listening to music reduces heart rate, respiratory rate, and blood pressure.

"ear drum," which in turn connects to the brain via nerve lines. This is a wealth of information, which affects and impresses us deeply. Regardless of what space we are in, when we hear a person speak, that person actually touches our innermost organs and our brain. Moreover, sound may be felt as a very intimate experience, sometimes more intimate and delicate than a kiss or a hug. Some may be attracted to and even fall in love with a person merely because of the sound of his or her voice.

Yuval Ron telling a story to his audience

Often during a post-concert reception, people tell me how the music I perform is a healing experience for them. And once in a while, someone may add that when I speak and tell a story or give some explanation in between the songs, my voice "nourishes the soul." As the Director of the Music Division at the Boston Conservatory, Dr. Karl Paulnack points out, "Being a musician involves taking on a great responsibility. With the right sound at the right time, a musician may be able to cure a wounded heart, a confused mind, a lost soul, or some physical pain."[72]

And the opposite also is true. Exposing ourselves to aggressive and oppressive music may lead to violent behavior and poor health. In 2012, a horrific murderous act against innocent Sikh Temple worshippers in the United States was linked to the murderer's prior participation in aggressive, hateful musical expression. While this link was merely speculation, recent social and neurological studies have shown that the wrong sound at the wrong time may lead to abuse and ill health.[73]

And language is sound, too. The power of words to positively and negatively impact human health has been documented in several recent studies, including neurological research which suggests that the use of words can affect the structure of the human brain.[74] Almost one hundred years ago, the Sufi master Hazrat Inayat Khan pointed to this phenomenon when he said, "The one who knows the chemistry of the word does not need drugs or herbs. He has medicine for every disease in the world, not only for bodily disease but also for the disorders of the

---

72 Quote by Karl Paulnack, D.M.A., currently Dean of the School of Music at Ithaca College, from a speech he gave to the parents of music students at New England Conservatory in Boston.

73 Various studies of adolescent smoking and drinking have established a connection between preferences for heavy metal, rap, reggae, techno music, and substance use. See "The Soundtrack of Substance Use: Music Preference and Adolescent Smoking and Drinking," by Prof. J. Mulder, Dept. of General Social Sciences, University of Utrecht, The Netherlands (2009). Furthermore, recent studies on the effects of music on heart rate and cardiovascular health have shown that violent or aggressive musical expressions, such as heavy metal and techno, may be dangerous for one's health and can lead to stress and/or life-threatening irregular heartbeats (see also studies by H.J. Trappe, M.D., Dept. of Cardiology and Angiology, University of Bochum, Herne, Germany).

74 See the book *Words Can Change Your Brain*, by Andrew Newburg, M.D. and Mark Robert Waldman.

mind, which still remain unexplored by science. By a constant study of life, by special thought given to one's words, by careful watching of the effects of one's speech upon others, one arrives at a state of realization where one can heal hearts."[75]

One of the earliest accounts we have about the healing power of sound is mentioned in the Hebrew Bible. This three thousand year-old testimony is one of the earliest, if not the most ancient, accounts of how sound heals mental illness. The biblical narrative describes the case of the first king of Israel, who oversaw a Middle Eastern nation that introduced the concept of the unity of all things, the unity of the Divine, and the concept of God as Oneness.[76] The Israelites were initiated as a spiritual nation led by prophets rather than kings. Under military pressure from neighboring tribes that all had kings, the Israelites demanded a king of their own. So with great reluctance, the spiritual leader of that time, Shmuel (Samuel), picked a young man named Shaul (Saul), anointed him, and made him the very first king of Israel.

Unfortunately, young King Saul had no experience on how to rule or by what means to hold together a nation that had never had a king before. As a result, the king often was depressed. None of the doctors could help. Then the king's advisors learned of a young shepherd up in the mountains around Jerusalem, who played beautiful music that enchanted animals and humans alike. The court quickly asked the shepherd's father for permission to bring the young musician to play for the depressed king. The young shepherd brought along his lute, his harp and a reed pan flute, and as soon as he began to play, the king's mood changed. Magically, his depression vanished and the king was cured of

---

75 From *The Sufi Message of Hazrat Inayat Khan: The Gathas,* Vol. 13, Part II, Gatha III, Section 3 (*circa* 1920) (www.spiritual-learning.com/message_14/13c.html).

76 The core statement in Judaism is: *Shema Israel Adonai Eloheinu Adonai Echad* ("Listen Israel, our Lord, our God, our Lord is ONE"). This directive is found in the Hebrew Bible (Deuteronomy 6:4).

his condition! The young shepherd was so beloved by the king that he was asked to remain at the court as a musician. Indeed, he became the first music therapist we know of in the Middle East. We don't know what kind of music the shepherd played or which musical scale or mode he used. In addition, there is no way to learn the details of King Saul's mental illness. The Hebrew Bible reveals, however, that music managed to cure Israel's first king on a regular basis. Later, the young music therapist would become probably the most famous king of Israel – King David – from whose lineage the Messiah would eventually come (according to Judeo-Christian traditions). Thus, during biblical times a long, long time ago, humans already knew the power of sound.

In even earlier times, according to the Hindu tradition, sound was used in similar ways, for medicinal purposes. This ancient knowledge, which also was discovered in China and Central Asia, has been kept alive by Indian yogis, mystics, and doctors despite attempted suppression by political institutions at home and the dominance of Western sciences abroad.[77] Now this wisdom is being re-channeled into a relatively new Western discipline, namely music therapy.

Another ray of hope is a new area of inquiry called Medical Ethnomusicology, which is an extension of Medical Anthropology. Scholars in this field are attempting to document and help preserve the historical, indigenous use of sound for healing, which is still being practiced by tribal societies around the globe. By merging this ancient human knowledge with current brain

---

77 See the work of M. Hari Haaren, Ph.D., Chairman of the Indian Music Therapy Research & Development Foundation in Kerala, India (www.Indian-MusicTherapy.org.in), and the work of Rahmi Oruc Guvenc, Ph.D., of the Tumata Society in Turkey (www.Tumata.com).

research, music therapy has the potential to expand our abilities to cure people through harmonic musical vibrations. You may find the right sound, the appropriate music that will promote the health of your body and positively affect your emotions and your states of mind. You may bathe in such sound, listening to the music playing very softly in the background while doing a task or while falling asleep. You may focus your complete attention on the music, dance to it, or receive body-work such as acupuncture and massage while music reinforces the healing process.[78] You also may experiment with meditating on sound, a practice that not only will improve your health, but also will provide an arena for studying your internal world, the nature of your being, and consequently help you develop inner peace. Using sound as a focus of meditation opens a vast window into the worlds of yoga, meditation and self study, *especially* for those people who have a hard time sitting still in order to meditate.[79]

Lastly, the power of sound goes well beyond its use as a tool for healing and well-being. The early spiritual masters of India determined that the world *is* sound, rhythm, and vibration (*Nada Brahma*). In recent times, scientists working within the disciplines of physics, math, logic, geometry and neuroscience have begun to confirm step-by-step that this is not a myth but rather a hidden unifying principle underlying *all* reality.[80]

---

78 To listen to music composed by Yuval Ron for medical and healing purposes, see: www.MettaMindfulnessMusic.com.

79 To experience sound meditation exercises and learn more about the therapeutic and mystical aspects of sound meditation, see Appendix A, "Yoga of Sound."

80 See the book *The World Is Sound: Nada Brahma: Music and the Landscape of Consciousness,* by Joachim-Ernst Berendt.

Hazrat Inayat Khan, the first master to introduce the Sufi wisdom of India to the West, concluded, "What makes us feel drawn to music is that our whole being is music – our mind and body, the nature in which we live, the nature which has made us, all that is beneath and around us – it is *all* music."[81]

---

81 From *The Music of the Spheres*, by Hazrat Inayat Khan.

CHAPTER XV

Father Bruno

*All the darkness in the world cannot put out
one small candle.*

~ Saint Francis of Assisi

*...and one small candle, reflected in many mirrors,
can light the whole world.*

~ Yuval Ron

Up in ancient hills leading to Jerusalem, there is a beautiful village called "Oasis of Peace."[82] In this blossoming village, Jewish, Christian, and Muslim families have endeavored to carry on a sacred mission: All are expected to remain faithful to their religious traditions while respecting those of others, and all are encouraged to dedicate their lives to advancing peace.

---

82 *Neve Shalom* in Hebrew; *Wahat el Salam* in Arabic.

While their brothers and sisters all around them have suffered continuous bloodshed, hate and war, *these people*, in this one village, have successfully resisted all hostilities. They have fruitfully kept their youth out of trouble, and they have accomplished this using conflict resolution counsels, dialogue, mediation, meditation, and prayer practices.

In this small village, all the children learn both Hebrew and Arabic, and all the children study the history and traditions of three Abrahamic faiths.[83] While many countries have schools for the art of war, in this village there is a school dedicated to the *art of peace*, since "peace is not spontaneous, it has to be learned."[84]

The story of this village sounds like a fairytale, but it is a true reality. It began as a dream of one monk named Father Bruno.[85] Bruno was born in the metropolis of Cairo, Egypt, where the great Nile River finally drains into the Mediterranean Sea. When he was very young, little Bruno already had a peculiar, innate notion that everything in life has some meaning. Every creature has a specific role. Every bee, every ant, every bird, and every little worm is somehow important. He knew that each living being had a meaningful role to play; only he did not know what the role of little Bruno was to be. So he kept on searching and wondering ...

When his family moved to France, Bruno kept looking for this answer. Then one day when he was eighteen or nineteen years old, Bruno met a group of Dominican monks who truly fascinated him with their gentleness and kindness. Suddenly, it

---

83 Judaism, Christianity, and Islam.

84 Father Bruno Hussar (1911-1996), from his autobiography, *When the Cloud Lifted*.

85 This rendering of Father Bruno's story is based on personal interviews, various publications, and news stories about Oasis of Peace and Father Bruno's life. It is an artistic retelling and not an historical account. Bruno's autobiography is the best source for an historical narrative of his amazing life.

became clear to him that he had concluded his quest! He finally discovered a framework, a path, a meaningful calling. Bruno was overjoyed! And he decided to take the vows to become a Christian monk.

That evening Bruno came home and said, "Mama, I found it! Today I vowed to become a monk. Finally, I found my life purpose!"

His mother began to cry.

"Mama, why are you crying? This is the happiest day of my life!"

His mother mournfully replied, "Oh Bruno, you are Jewish. We are all Jewish. We had to keep it a secret ... because of the times."

Suddenly the world collapsed in front of Bruno's eyes. Everything that seemed clear and certain shattered into pieces. He didn't know who he was: *Am I an Arab from Egypt? A Jew from France? Or a Catholic Dominican monk?*

And then he saw an opening, a light out of the darkness. In an instant, he knew that the answer *must* be found in the Holy Land, for that is where all these identities, all three of these religions have mingled together for over a thousand years. The answer to who he really is would be waiting for him over there!

As Bruno boarded the ship heading to the East, he knew this sacred pilgrimage would change his life. Once he landed in Israel, he hurried to visit the holy city of Jerusalem, but on the way something else caught his eye. It was an old monastery set in heavy stone, lying halfway between the Mediterranean Sea and the mountains. This was the old "Silent Monastery," where monks vow to never, ever speak again. This is their path; this is their sacred journey.

Bruno was moved and inspired. He felt he might be happy at that monastery, and indeed he was. He was pleased to be silent and to be of service. He worked in the vegetable garden. He grew vegetables out of the sacred ground that gave birth to the great traditions of Abraham and Jesus, and he took joy in feeding his brothers the monks. Finally, Bruno felt he had found the meaning of his life.

But late one night while he was asleep, Bruno had a terrible nightmare. An unearthly, loud voice came into his head and said, "Bruno, you *must* find a way to help Jews, Christians, and Muslims live in peace on this Holy Land. Bruno, you have to find a way to make this true!"

Bruno woke up covered in a cold sweat. *What can I do?* he thought. *How can I, a simple monk, accomplish such an impossible decree?* Then a vision magically unfolded in his mind: *A village! I can start a village! A village where the sons and daughters of Abraham may live together on this sacred land and serve as an example of peace for the whole world!*

With this grand vision in his feverish mind and with an incredible rush of energy, Bruno ran down the hallway of the monastery, where he saw the headmaster standing in deep contemplation. Bruno reached over, grabbed the headmaster by his shoulders, and cried, "Father, I *must* speak to you!"

So ended Bruno's career in the silent monastery.

But the headmaster was a kind man, and he knew that Bruno had more important work to do than growing vegetables and staying silent. He knew that Bruno's life had a larger meaning and that Bruno had a different role to play. So the headmaster granted Bruno's wish and assigned to him a whole side of the hill on the path to Jerusalem, which the monastery had owned for many years.

Yet, the land he gave Bruno was bare; it had no water, no trees, and no roads. Undaunted, Bruno took a large crate, cut a door into it, and set it on top of the bare hill – it was his first cabin. For several years, nobody followed him up that barren hill. Then finally, five families agreed to join him, and they began to turn the dream into a reality.

Today, the village is thriving and there is a long waiting list of families who want to move there. Families from neighboring villages now send their children to study at the school in the village, because they too want their children to be educated in an Oasis of Peace. People from all over the world, who work for non-governmental organizations and the United Nations, now go to study at the School of Peace in Bruno's village. They come to be trained in the methods and practices that Father Bruno and the residents of Oasis of Peace have been utilizing all these years. They come to learn from the people of the village in order to bring peace to other troubled regions around the globe. Associations called "Friends of Oasis of Peace" now exist in eleven different countries, and numerous individuals now take inspiration from the courage, endurance, and methodologies that the village has put forth.

When Father Bruno died, his friends discovered an envelope on his desk. The entire village gathered around. They knew this document had to be Father Bruno's last will and testament. They opened the envelope, took the letter out, and read Bruno's last words, his final teaching:

> *Friends, you thought this project of ours was about tolerance. You thought it was about co-existence among Jews and Arabs. You thought it was about mediation and non-violent conflict resolution. These were merely tools, my friends. In truth, this project of ours was about Love.*

CHAPTER XVI

Pursuing Peace

The 19th Century Italian composer Rossini once said, "There are only two kinds of music: good and bad." American jazz legends Duke Ellington and Louis Armstrong (and some say Frank Zappa as well) often repeated this statement publicly. What they referred to as "good music" can be described as music that is an authentic expression of beauty, harmony, and truth.[86] Yet music also can serve as a bridge to a higher purpose beyond itself, and such is the case with the music my ensemble has been spreading throughout the world for the past three decades.

Believe it or not, the Yuval Ron Ensemble was not formed for musical or artistic purposes. Rather, I formed the ensemble with the intent that it be an educational tool to promote and inspire social action. I recall that during our first radio interview, the host read to his listeners our original mission statement: *To foster better understanding of Middle Eastern cultures and religions.*

---

86 For further discussion on beauty, harmony and truth, see Chapter VIII, "On the Nature of Harmonious Sound and Beauty."

At the time, my desire was to inform audiences about the complex yet underlying common cultural bond that many people of the Middle East share. It was a little step in forging positive change in the world, a small investment in our future, an effort to use music, dance and education to build a better world for our children.

Often I am asked about the impact of my ensemble's work on the prospect of peace in the Middle East. This is a difficult question to answer, because the process that artists are involved in is a slow one. I once told a reporter, "Imagine having a huge territory, a dusty piece of land with no trees, no shade, and very few plants. There's no way to magically snap your fingers and get some fruit trees growing out of it. All we can do is to move one inch at a time, step-by-step, and sow more and more seeds, nurture them, and hope they grow. That's all any of us can do. Healing the wounds, putting the past behind us, and bringing about justice and forgiveness are lofty goals to achieve in one generation; it probably won't happen in my lifetime. Hopefully, however, I am contributing to measurable shifts in the consciousness of the masses and helping to usher in a more compassionate world – one without regard to nationality, race, financial status, or level of education."

I was born and raised in Israel. During my youth, I had no relationships with Arabs, Christians, or Muslims. The culture I was raised in taught me to view Arabs as my fierce opponents. Later in life, my work with the Yuval Ron Ensemble led me to collaborate with and befriend many artists of the Arabic world, both Christians and Muslims. Today when I meet artists from countries that traditionally oppose my homeland, I first connect to the humanity in them, rather than the exterior layers of nationality or race. Then it is possible to delight in sharing many passions: for music, cuisine, and culture that are unique to the Middle Eastern lands we come from.

Even more exciting is when we create something together, such as a new song, dance, or other artistic work. And it is absolute bliss to then share what we have created with the public! Those projects which reach beyond borders prove that it is possible to overcome adverse elements – on both sides – that crave to perpetuate darkness. For me, these collaborations are a great source of hope ... and an emanation of the Light.

The Light finds its expression on many levels. Just one enlightened leader such as Mahatma Gandhi or one advanced artist such as Peter Gabriel can impact millions of people over many generations. Such cultural and spiritual evolution can be initiated from the outside, as through the arts, education, and mentorship, or it may arise independently within an individual. Ultimately, peace is a natural outcome of the true realization of the Oneness of all life forms. And I believe this realization will be achieved by a majority of humanity one day, after which we will collectively experience true peace on our planet.

The great 16ᵗʰ Century Jewish Kabbalistic master Rabbi Yitzchak Luria taught that the state of the world is "brokenness," but that this is a temporary state. The world can be and should be repaired. And each one of us has a role in repairing our broken world, by sharing creativity, joy, and never-ending determination.

We, the artists, strive to find creative, beautiful solutions for problems within our spheres of influence. This is our sacred commitment. Some of our greatest composers, such as Mahler and Beethoven, worked on a single symphony for ten, fifteen, even thirty years! These masters struggled for long periods of time to find the perfect solution that would keep their symphonic work in harmony, with an appropriate balance of elements and narratives, a balance that would render it a whole, complete work.

This heightened level of commitment and creative problem-solving ought to inspire the many efforts to provide solutions for the many challenges we face in the 21ˢᵗ Century: economic, ecological, political, cultural, and spiritual. Reforming our civilization into a more just and sustainable model is a prerequisite for achieving stable, lasting, and peaceful coexistence. And the arts shall continue to inspire and promote this process. That is the true meaning of the work I do with my ensemble.[87]

At this critical moment in human history, I have come to believe that producing "good music" is not enough. The wailing of humanity and the waning of earth are cries for good music that also has the power to help repair our world.

---

87   For more information regarding the social activism of the Yuval Ron Ensemble, please see the list of past benefit performances listed on our Calendar page (www.yuvalronmusic.com/calendar/past-benefits.html).

Chapter XVII

Can a Song Heal?

Sometimes in life we plan to accomplish something, and for that reason we set upon a path that may lead us to a completely unexpected attainment.

In 2007, my ensemble and I led a "Peace Mission" tour to Israel. Accompanying us were thirty people from around the world who wished to participate in that extraordinary journey. We visited several villages and towns in Israel, where we met some brave people who would never be written about in the world press, folks who were trying to do the right thing: artists, educators, and activists who work tirelessly to bring Jews and Arabs together, to sow the seeds of peace. We embarked on this adventure in order to support, inspire, and energize these courageous pioneers.

Seeking thresholds of light led us to a small village nested in the hills leading to Jerusalem. This prosperous village is the home of Jewish, Christian, and Muslim families that choose to live together in equality and a peacefully integrated life. As the quiet ancient hills around them carry memories of biblical past, the pastoral air over them reassures that here exists an oasis, a point of stillness in the midst of the eye of constant storms and conflicts.

I learned of the village only a few years earlier, from a young British director who was making a film about it. "The music from your CD *Under the Olive Tree* [88] magically fit as the soundtrack to my film!" she announced over the phone. "Would you please grant us the rights to use it?" I asked to see the film first, and afterward I gladly granted the rights for the use of my music and donated my licensing fees to the village.

Now I was finally here – on the grounds of this oasis – walking through the village and hearing its story first-hand. My ensemble was with me as we offered a musical presentation for the village families at their Spiritual Center. All we hoped for was to give them support, to share a similar harmony with our music and dance, to show them they weren't alone.

That evening, the villagers filled the large stone house that serves as their Spiritual Center. Families, couples, and individuals all mingled among the thirty supporters who travelled with us on the tour. When we started playing music, all the children began to dance. *What a beautiful moment*, I thought to myself, as I realized that I couldn't tell which of the children were Jewish, which were Christian, or which were Muslim. They were simply kids, dancing joyfully together and celebrating a place beyond borders and separations.

There was great joy and happiness in the room. I glanced at the two adorable children who came along with us from the United States – one Asian-American and the other Jewish-American – and they were dancing playfully with the children of the village. It was *everything* that we had hoped for.

---

88 You may hear *Under the Olive Tree* at: www.cdbaby.com/cd/yuval.

But then, I noticed a man and a woman sitting in the last row, staring at me with a bleak gaze as though I were doing something wrong. I was in the middle of a song, yet I decided to put my oud down on the stage, walk through the audience, and approach this couple. I stood next to them and asked if they would like us to stop the music. Neither the man nor his wife even looked at me; they just kept staring straight ahead. Then, in a low and monotone voice the man said, "Keep playing."

Somewhat bewildered, I turned around and headed back to the stage. I took up my oud and we kept on playing.

Only a few minutes after this bizarre event, another unexpected twist unfolded. A woman who came all the way from Holland to join our tour approached me and said with forceful voice, "You simply *must* play that old Israeli song about love, the song that the Sufi Ruhaniat Order[89] recently adapted and turned into a chant for peace using the Hebrew word *shalom* and the Arabic word *salam*.[90] You must play it right now. This is the moment and this is the place!"

"Look," I said, "I know this song from my childhood, having grown up in Israel, but my ensemble members don't know it. So there is no way we could play it now, I am sorry. It's not part of our repertoire."

She repeated again, with an incredibly vigorous conviction, "You *must* play it right *now!*"

I sensed a powerful, invisible wind, a powerful energy confronting me, and I quickly decided to go along with it. Turning to my musicians, I said, "Just do your best to follow along," and I began playing the song. The musicians were amazing; they

---

89 Within Sufism, which is the mystical path within Islam, there are various groups or Orders (*Tarikat* in Arabic). The Ruhaniat Order is an offshoot of Hazrat Inayat Khan's Sufi Order International and the Chishti Sufi lineage.

90 Both words are translated as "peace."

picked up the tune in few seconds and accompanied me, as if they knew the song by heart.

People started singing along with us – "*Shalom, Salam*" – as we began playing the song faster and faster. The villagers formed two circles and danced and danced, singing and chanting the word "peace" in their native tongues of Hebrew and Arabic, a word that reflected the essence of their life's long undertaking.

I looked up toward the back row, searching for the gloomy couple. They still were sitting at the rear of the room, frozen as ice. Suddenly the woman – the one who had been glaring at me for so long – jumped up with a fire-colored scarf in her hand and ran into the circle! She held that scarf fiercely, as she started to dance in the middle of the circle. And she moved in an ecstatic fiery rhythm. She was an incredible dancer! She appeared as a flame in the middle of that circle, dancing for her life.

At the end of the concert, her husband walked slowly from the back of the room, straight toward me. He came close and whispered in a low and exhausted voice, "This was very difficult for us. It was hard for my wife to sit and not dance. But it was painful for her to dance too …." He then paused and uttered with incredible finality, "My wife hasn't danced for three years. She hasn't danced since we lost our daughter."

I looked at this bereaved father and then it dawned on me that we didn't just come to this oasis to support coexistence, dialogue, and tolerance. Yes, we came to inspire and support these people who had dedicated their lives to a serious experiment in the art of peace, people who had pledged themselves to the art of putting the past in the past, and building a future of peace and prosperity for their children. Surely, we warmed their hearts and gave them additional energy with which to go forward and upward …

However, on a much deeper level, we had a more profound purpose for being in the village that night, one we had not anticipated: We came to free an imprisoned, grieving soul and to open a healing window for the life force to enter. We were there to mend one broken heart with a song.[91]

---

91 The song is "Erev Shel Shoshanim/Shalom-Salam," as recorded for the first time in Hebrew and Arabic by the Yuval Ron Ensemble on the CD *Seeker of Truth*. You may hear the song at: www.cdbaby.com/cd/yuval9.

CHAPTER XVIII

Beyond Concerts

One of the great moments I experienced with my ensemble was in 2008, when we gave a concert at Benaroya Hall in Seattle, a fine concert hall and home of the Seattle Symphony. When the concert ended, we were ushered into a post-concert reception hosted by Seattle University, which was our host for the city-wide residency.

The president of the university took the podium. This fine man – a Jesuit priest who has a doctorate in spirituality – captured in words the vision I always hold in my heart and mind before I start a concert, even though I have never expressed it publicly, nor heard or read it anywhere. He started by searching for the exact words and the appropriate adjectives to convey what he felt during the concert. As I recall, he said, "I don't know how to describe what we have just experienced. This was not a concert; this was an event beyond what one would expect from a mere concert. This was a …." He then paused as he grappled for the right words, "It was a meditation … an experience … a prayer."

His words seemed to resonate with all of the people in the hall, especially with me, since they captured what I always intend to create at every concert and every lecture demonstration that I present.

And then he said something even more amazing – a statement I will never forget! He told the audience of fellow faculty, administrators, board members, and university supporters, "I feel that by being here, at this concert, I've done my prayers for the whole week!" Everyone laughed and expanded their hearts just a bit wider.

Indeed, my concerts are not meant to be just entertaining. What is more important for me is that they expand the musical experience into an educational opportunity, a prayer, a community gathering, an energetic, purifying and deeply *transformative* experience. For us, the artists, these concerts are certainly a form of sacred ritual. That is why I ask my ensemble performers to always dress in white, the color of purity, the one color that "accepts all," because when all the colors in the spectrum are combined, they produce the color white. It is a color that brings to mind various ancient traditions of sacred worship.[92] It is the color associated with the ethereal, metaphysical realms and with the quality of pure light.[93]

One of the most pleasurable moments for me on a tour is when I meet the audience at the end of the concert. After the last encore, we make a point of staying in the theater so we can personally greet the audience in the lobby. We love to meet the community, to hug, to exchange kind words or encourage a young fan, to answer questions, to share stories, to ask questions, and to hear how the music has transformed their moods and elevated their souls.

---

92 The *Kohanim* (priests) in the Jerusalem Temple wore white, as did many priests, imams, and shamans in East.

93 There are many references in Kabbalah, the mystical teaching of Judaism, about white light representing the highest world, the Source of Creation, God, and the royal element in Creation (*Keter* in the Tree of Life).

Sometimes, we end up dining and celebrating with audience members following the concerts. In several rural areas and in faraway places such as Alaska, people are extremely generous with us, and their hospitality reminds me of the "Old World" hospitality of the Middle East. This ancient custom of sharing, which you may still find in the desert lands, was once rooted in the belief that the guest is a manifestation of God and that he or she deserves protection, shelter, and the *best of the best*.

We also keep in touch with some of the people we meet on the road and become lasting friends. We exchange ideas and information, inspire and support each other, as we continue to enrich each other's lives. This is truly an amazing outcome of our concert tours.

This rewarding outreach was not part of my life during the start of my career, when I was working exclusively as a professional composer of music for film, TV, contemporary dance, theatre, and art installations. For many years, all my work was done inside music studios, and I had very little contact with audiences or with communities. At that time, I felt my work as a composer did bring beauty and harmony to film projects and TV programs, while also making them more effective. Yet, I did not feel my music had direct impact on the lives of people and the state of the world.

So in 1999, I took it upon myself to venture out of the studio, to begin teaching and sharing stories of Middle Eastern history and culture, wisdom tales that I had collected during my years of researching music and mysticism. What I wished to create were experiences that would inspire people and make a difference in their lives. For me, this is social and political work that I express through music and education. It is a calling which grew stronger and stronger inside of me, while my rational mind was telling me to focus on my stable and safe career as a composer.

During my concerts, I often witness transformations taking place within the audience. I watch the people entering the concert hall and sitting down. Most of them don't talk to others they don't know, and I observe how they relate to each other as separated individuals. Yet, as the concert progresses, they begin to interact with me and each other, and by the end of the concert, it seems we are all one big happy family! I cannot express how deeply it moves me to see people looking at each other with empathy in their eyes, people of different races smiling and hugging strangers whom they previously might have called "foreigners."

Similarly, in post-concert receptions, I notice people who didn't know each other before the concert beaming with a new light as they talk, share, and compare their experience. There is a warmth that wasn't there before the concert began. Often people want to linger in the lobby. They simply don't want to go home, back to an individualistic existence and the experience of separation. In fact, several times people have contacted me to say that a concert changed their lives. "It was a transformative experience for me, thank you so much!" they exclaim.

I understand what they are feeling. I know that during a concert, the music brings down barriers, it melts a cold layer, the protective barrier that we put up as we grow older. After the concert, everyone seems to radiate an aura of warmth and beauty, and they want to stay in that atmosphere and hold on tight to the light. That is the beginning of an even grander experience, the moment a seed is sown for personal and social change.

And so over the years of touring with the Yuval Ron Ensemble, it has become clear to me that the word "concert" is too narrow to describe what we performers and the audience receive during these blessed experiences. As one sophisticated man told me in a post-concert reception, "This was *not* a concert. This was an invocation for awaking our higher virtues!" What a remarkable way to relate an indescribable emotion, the inspiration we all feel at the end of our concert. No doubt, it is beyond mere music. It is a peak experience, much like the altered states of mind and higher consciousness attained through deep meditation and prayer. As the great master violinist and conductor Yehudi Menuhin once pointed out:

> *Music is a therapy.*
> *It is a communication*
> *far more powerful than words,*
> *far more immediate,*
> *far more efficient.*

Yuval feels the bond with his audience

CHAPTER XIX

A Promise in the
Midst of Catastrophe

I was asked to present an interfaith concert at the prestigious All Saints Church, a stunning gothic revival Episcopal church located just east of downtown Los Angeles. My plan was to stage a festive production featuring two spectacular, liturgical female dancers in exquisite costumes, my two lead female singers, and the full Yuval Ron Ensemble.

Tragically, an earthquake shook the island of Haiti just a few weeks before the event, and horrible images of death and destruction were televised around the world. As the concert date got closer and closer, I began to contemplate what I could say to the audience to help all of us find a way to cope with the disaster. What story could I tell that might lift people's spirits at such a difficult time?

Then I came across an article about a young American photographer who found himself in the midst of a different earthquake – the one that shook Armenia about twenty-five years ago. His story suddenly allowed me to see points of light in the current Haitian catastrophe, because even though the *suffering was great on the island, the counter stream of compassion and support for the Haitians was reaching a spectacular level. Doctors from all over the world were travelling to the disaster zone to provide a helping hand. Some had never been trained to work in such frustrating and compromised situations, but the doctors were doing heroic work, as were all the other volunteers from around the world.*

Keeping the earthquake victims and volunteers in my mind and heart, I went on stage on January 31, 2011, at the All Saints Church in Pasadena. I told the audience the following story of a photographer's courageous acts during the 1988 Armenian earthquake, and I dedicated the story to the outstanding human beings who were helping Haiti and to the "Armenian Quarter" of my ensemble: Norik Manoukian, Virginie Alimian and Yeghish Manukyan, all of whom are magnificent musicians with amazing hearts!

A terrible earthquake hit Armenia in 1988. Many people died and many houses were destroyed. In the midst of all the mayhem and destruction, there was a young American photographer who happened to be there on vacation, and he began to chronicle the disaster.

At first, he ran around on foot – from ruin to ruin – taking photos. Then, he asked an Armenian driver to take him to other disaster locations. Day and night, he waded through a landscape of dead bodies and ruined houses taking pictures. And day and night, he managed to email his photos to all his contacts, so the world could see the extent of the tragedy and hopefully respond.

During their fifth night on the road, the photographer and his driver saw an old man waving wildly and blocking the road. The driver stopped and began speaking with the man, but the photographer could not understand what they were saying. The Armenian driver interpreted in English, "This man says he lost his wife … and his four children in the horrible quake … and the bodies are still under the rubble where his house used to stand. All he has left after the disaster are his pants, a scarf, and the coat he is wearing. He is asking if we will take him to his village so that he may find the bodies of his wife and children."

The young photographer had been in war zones before and he'd photographed dead bodies before, but he had never seen or been part of anything as horrific as this. The young man quickly opened the rear door of the car and motioned for the old man to sit next to him in the back seat. Then off they went.

It was a cold, rainy night. The three men drove in silence through a dark landscape of corpses and flattened houses. The American was exhausted; he hadn't slept in four nights. Instead, he'd been working around the clock on a job no one had assigned him.

His head was getting heavier and heavier, and his eyes were slowly closing in spite of himself. He just couldn't stay awake any longer. And as his eyes closed, his head began to sway. Left and right he swayed … right and left … slowly falling asleep on this cold, rainy, and dreadful night.

Suddenly, he felt a hand on his head. Then the hand was supporting his head, a strong hand that began gently pushing his head down, down, down, to the old man's lap. It was the hand of the old man – a man he didn't know at all – and now the hand was caressing his hair.

The photographer just lay there, in the car, being driven to God knows where. He could feel the old man caressing his hair, and he began to feel awkward, strange. It was a weird experience. He didn't know this old man, this stranger who was caressing his hair.

Through the haze of his fatigued mind, the American unexpectedly sensed the deep meaning of this bizarre scene. The old man – who had lost *everything* – needed at that moment to touch another human being. So the moment wasn't about him, the young photographer. It wasn't *for* him. So he made an effort to relax every muscle in his body and to let go of his anxiety. He dared to let this experience flow through him for the sake of the old man.

And then he heard the old man singing in a thin yet tender voice. He sang an Armenian folk song, and for a few minutes, the sound of the rain and the pulsating engine and the old folk song all blended into a sweet serenade. The photographer floated as if inside a magical dream, an oasis of sound in the midst of a broken world. And the old man continued to sing the entire time they drove to his ruined house, the crumbled quarters that still hid the dead bodies buried beneath it.

By the time they finally arrived at village, the rain had stopped. The old man got out of the car and approached what was left of his house – now just a ruin covering lifeless bodies. He fell to the ground crying and kissing the earth.

The American photographer looked at the old man with a fatigued and impatient gaze. He had a lot of work to do. He had numerous photos to transfer into his computer and send out to the world. He needed to get back into the car and head to the hotel … but he found he just couldn't. He couldn't leave the old man there alone. So he continued to stand there, along with his Armenian driver. They both stood and waited, watching the old man cry and kiss the land that had been shaken, the land that felled his house, crushing and burying his wife and children.

The night had gotten colder and colder. Eventually, the old man stood up, turned around, and looked at the American. The young photographer was shivering. And as if he were having a daydream or watching a slow-motion video, he saw the old man take off his scarf and hand it to the driver. "The American is cold … give him my scarf," he uttered slowly.

The driver complied and placed the scarf on the young photographer. The scarf felt good and warm, but it was not right. The American had a warm hotel bed waiting for him. So he took the scarf off and he put it back around the neck of the old man. But the old man protested, and he again removed the scarf and put it around the young photographer's neck, saying to the interpreter, "Tell the American, it is very cold and he needs it more than I do."

As this surreal scene unfolded in front of his exhausted eyes, the young photographer became more and more uncomfortable with the old man's kindness. But once again, he allowed compassion to flood his senses, just as he had in the car when the man stroked his head. Then suddenly, he understood the true meaning of the gift.

The scarf was not the gift, for what he received from this old man would stay with him for the rest of his life. The gift was a pure inner-faith, a trustful confidence, and a reassurance in the human spirit. The gift was a promise that even in the face of the worst catastrophe, there exists an even greater expression of human connectedness and compassion, an even greater expression of love.

CHAPTER XX

Moses and the Young Shepherd

Those of us who grew up within the Judeo-Christian tradi-
tions are familiar with many biblical stories about Moshe
Rabeynu (in Hebrew, "Moses our spiritual teacher"). Yet many
of us are not aware of the various stories about Nabi Musa
("Prophet Moses" in Arabic) that exist within the Islamic and
Sufi traditions. One of these beautiful Sufi teaching stories –
which Rumi also retold – has been carried forth within the
Hassidic Jewish tradition, as well. Yet in the Hassidic version,
Moses is not mentioned at all. Instead, the role of the sinning
spiritual leader is given to an anonymous rabbi, and the consequence of his sin is death. In the Sufi story, which I render
below, Moses' blunder leads him to learn important lessons,
and he becomes much wiser as a result.

One day, Moses was walking on the dunes of the mystical Sinai desert. As far and near as the eye could see, there was sand … and just sand … and more sand. It was as if the world were an ocean of yellow waves of silky sand.

The warm desert wind blew quietly over the dunes, and through the whisper of the wind, Moses heard another sound – a reed flute! A beautiful and enchanting tune was carried to his ears, and he could not help but follow the sound.

He walked toward the enticing music. It seemed that the reed flute tune came from behind one of the curvy hills of sand. Past that dune, Moses could see a desert bush, out of which emanated the hypnotic sound. Now, Moses became pensive. *Who was playing this flute?* In spite of himself, he approached the magical, musical bush.

Suddenly, the unseen reed flute stopped whistling. Moses stopped in his tracks. He heard a voice. Behind the bush he saw a young shepherd boy talking to himself. Moses turned around to leave, but then a greater force within him pushed him forward, toward the bush, toward the shepherd boy who was still holding a reed flute in his hands. The boy was young, maybe fourteen, at most sixteen years old. Moses got close enough so he could make sense of what the boy was saying. The young shepherd was talking to God.

Moses was not used to eavesdropping on private conversations, but a strange force within him refused to let him retreat. He felt as though his whole being was attracted to this young boy, and he could not help but listen with intense attention to that young voice.

"Master of the Universe, I love you and all that you are. All your creation delights and amazes me. But, it is so difficult for me to be so far away from you. I long to see you. I desire to see you one time, just one time. It is such a weight for me to carry this great love for you without ever seeing you. If you could only come for a short visit, I would make some tea for you, tea with *naana*![94] I would give you a sugar cube, so you could put it in your mouth before you sip the tea. And then, as you drink the tea, it would mix with the sugar cube and ....."

Moses was stunned. *What was this ridiculous nonsense? This ignorant boy was raving mad!* But Moses could not stop himself from continuing to listen.

The young shepherd was going on again, "My God, the God of my ancestors, if you could just afford to pay me a brief visit, just for a little while, I would prepare for you my favorite lamb in salt and serve it to you on a tray full of flames. And while you dine, I would tell you the story about the young camel that was bitten by the long black snake, and after dinner, if you have time to rest, I would serve you with more mint tea and leisurely file your nails."

Moses couldn't stand it any longer ... he simply could not contain himself any more. He rushed around the bush toward the shepherd boy, grabbed him by the shoulders, and shook him as hard as he could. Moses was rarely accustomed to raising his voice, but now he shouted. "Don't you know? God is everywhere! Don't you know God cannot be seen? What do you mean by saying these ignorant words? Telling God to come for a *visit*? To have some *tea* with you? What are you *talking* about? God is an eternal Light! A Light all around you and inside of you – it is an *endless* Light!"

The boy started sobbing. He cried with awe, surprise, and shock. He cried with shame and confusion. He was totally crushed.

Moses backed off, as the atmosphere around him suddenly grew thick with unseen vibrations. It felt as though the air was full of particles, and that these particles carried tiny flames that were burning his face. A voice inside him began talking. He heard the voice addressing him:

---

94 Tea with fresh mint.

Moses ... what have you done?
You have distanced one of my lovers away from me.
You have crushed a young and tender soul.

Moses turned around. The young shepherd had vanished. All around him, Moses saw only dunes, and more dunes, and dunes of yellow sand that seemed to float in the wind, flying high about his head and low around his feet.

Then a quiet, gentle desert breeze began to cool his face. A new deep wisdom slowly formed within him. In that miraculous moment, Moses recognized a new revealed truth: *How one behaves in the world might be more important than the beliefs one holds dear.*

With every faith and with every belief, gentleness and tender care are warranted, for at the core of every spiritual tradition, there is a seed of true and innocent love – the spark of the Beloved.[95]

---

95 In Sufi terminology, the "Beloved" is a code word for the Divine Source of all life.

Chapter XXI

Embrace the Shadow

There is no point in fighting darkness with darkness;
All we need to do is to increase the Light.

It was Easter time, a time for the "Deer Dance." Nature was rebirthing itself when the native people of the Yaqui tribe[96] were about to enact a unique ritual drama. The stage was a large vacant, dusty field. At the end of this large sandy lot stood the little church of the Yaqui reservation. It was a mere empty shack under a simple wooden roof, yet it served as a place of worship. There was no floor in the church, for it was important for the Yaqui to feel the earth under their feet when they entered a sacred place.

My good friend Rabbi Michael, who has been a close friend of the Yaqui chief, insisted that I must experience the

---

96 The indigenous people of Northwestern Mexico, who later were dispersed over many parts of Mexico and the southwestern United States.

Deer Dance and see the beauty of a ritual which grew out of a sustainable civilization nested in nature. It was a sunny and warm April Sunday in the middle of spring time, and the bare, desolated reservation waited for some grace, for some magic.

The musicians were sitting on the sidelines of the large open lot. I could hear them playing the water drum (a gourd dipped in water). Layered over this indigenous music, Spanish-Christian songs were being chanted by another group of Yaqui musicians on the other side of the field. The two musical traditions blended in a strange counterpoint, as if they were part of a novel composition presented during an experimental music night, or at a major museum, or in a prestigious concert hall. The layered sound was hard to digest, however. I wished to hear only the Native water drum music or just the Spanish chants alone, but for the Yaqui, hearing the two streams of music simultaneously made perfect sense. That was their reality, and they embraced and completely owned both threads.

A man dressed as a deer entered the lot by the little church. He was a handsome, noble man, tall and lean, decorated with exquisite feathers and natural leather. He began to dance in beautiful, delicate movements, and I could feel the quality of a precious young and vulnerable deer moving a few feet from me.

On the other side of the empty field, a large group of young Yaqui men gathered to play the role of the "bad guys." Dressed in faded t-shirts and worn-out pants, there was nothing native or traditional about their appearance. Yet, they were ready to play their part. Convincing as they could be, they carried real weapons and live ammunition. On cue, they ran toward the deer dancer and began aiming their guns at the sky overhead. These guys looked tough and serious – even angry and violent! – as they ran down the hill toward the sacred and elegant deer dancer, who still pranced, unsuspecting, by the little church.

But the deer dancer was not alone. Directly in front of him was a congregation of old women, girls, boys, and elderly men. They were all dressed simply and casually, with no trace of native attire. They looked like any another small town community in a rural area. They stood there sweating under the sun, tense, and completely focused on the armed mob running down the hill toward them. And then they did the most fascinating and surprising thing: They ran into the wave of attackers and with their bare hands tried to catch any aggressor they could.

Although the attackers and the protectors were actually all one tribe, community members split along their assigned roles. Brothers grabbed fellow brothers, mothers ran to corral sons, and uncles strived to restrain angry nephews. And when they managed to catch an assailant, they would immediately pacify him with a strong sweaty embrace.

The subduers brought the attackers over to the side of the dancing deer, to the side of the Light, and ushered them into the little floorless church. All during the chaos, the deer dancer with his colorful feathers kept on moving gracefully, as if he were in a completely tranquil space – a place of beauty, freedom, and bliss.

But now a second assault ensued! This wave was even more violent and more ferocious than the first. The protectors boldly ran toward this angry mob, as if they were rushing into a stormy ocean in order to save a baby from a tidal wave. With incredible courage, they seized some of the violent attackers, encircled them, and gripped them tightly, which immediately disarmed the hostility. Then they took the pacified captives to the side of the sacred deer by the church. And the noble dancer, with his decorated legs, kept swaying without a pause, beaming the purity of nature and the intangible mystery of an infinite Light.

Then came the third wave. There were shots in the air, and I began wondering if people were truly about to get hurt. Nevertheless, the community – mothers and fathers, uncles and grandparents – ran into the dark eruption of youthful aggression and violence, took hold of the wild gang, and brought them down to the deer. Time after time, a miracle of transformation took place before my eyes. Firmly embracing the "enemy," the humble protectors brought their adversaries to the side of the illuminated deer, and the shadows evaporated piece-by-piece.[97]

This was a staged production, an Easter Sunday morning play, a "play within a play," as the mystics of the East would say. What a fascinating event!

In the intricate universal drama we call "Life" – as in the Deer Dance ritual – there exists a way to transform the shadows and darkness of humanity using the power of a full-hearted embrace. And for me, music is the path for such a transformative experience.

As I travel the world from community to community, as did the troubadours of old, I carry the spellbinding ritual of the Deer Dance in my heart. As a warrior of peace, I know and respect the shadow as an integral part of the foundations of our universe. I know brother Shadow is necessary in order to provide an existential context for the Light, in the same way the dark night ushers in the next sunny day. My hope is for balance between shadow and light, more deer dancers, and more transformative embraces – all of which helps fear-driven forces see the unity of all life. Being fully conscious of this unity will inevitably lead to peace.

---

97 In the original Deer Dance before the arrival of Spanish Christian people, the ritual ended with the deer sacrificing his life to the hunters, allowing the circle of life to continue. Animals, as metaphors, are abundant in folk dances of various cultures around the world. The deer is a Buddhist symbol, too. A male and female deer adorn the top of Tibetan monasteries and schools at either side of the Dharma wheel. Buddha first taught at Deer Park in India. Guru Padmasambhava, who came to Tibet from India, is said to ride a deer. Deer dances occur also in the Buddhist kingdom of Bhutan in South Asia, where the deer is a symbol of desire.

My efforts are a drop in the ocean, but I know for certain that the right sound, the right music can heal a bleeding heart and calm a restless soul. And so, even if the universe would end tomorrow, today I choose to keep on working to mend a broken world with an inspired sound ... to embrace the shadow and increase the Light ... one musical note at a time.

APPENDIX A

The Yoga of Sound
Three Exercises

Nada Yoga or Sound Yoga is an ancient Hindu practice which forms the foundation for the sound meditation workshops I have been leading over the years. For me, exploring the effects of sound on various people in different intimate settings has been a continuous research project. This work has been done in "laboratories" where we experiment with sound as a tool to reach the infinite realms of human spirituality and psychology. If you wish to try such inner explorations, please experiment with the three exercises outlined below.

Sound Meditation: Exercise One

This is a very basic, yet very important exercise. It is a meditation which focuses on the sound of a bell. You may use any bell, a singing bowl, or any object that produces some metallic ringing sound.

First, hold the bell and look at it. Then close your eyes, strike the bell, and listen to the sound. Just let the sound fill you completely. Let all your thoughts and images float away while holding onto the sound. Note how long the sound still exists in the space around you, and hold onto it in your consciousness, even as it fades away.

These moments of listening to the fading sound of a bell offer a very fine period of meditation. When you truly can no longer hear the receding sound of the bell, listen to the silence. Listen fully to all that you can hear. Take note of it without superimposing any judgment or commentary, as if you were simply an indifferent scientist collecting data.

Then strike the bell again. If a thought enters your mind or if an image appears, just look at it and say to it kindly and patiently in your mind: *I will think about you later. I'll get back to you later.* And then return your full attention to the ringing sound of the bell.

After you complete about ten minutes of this listening meditation, ask yourself some questions such as:

• Were there some moments when I was completely immersed in the sound?

• Was there any experience of losing myself in the sound, in other words, having moments of no thoughts, when I was completely listening to the sound to the point where the sound seemed to be inside of me?

• What happened during the periods of silence before the next strike of the bell?

It is interesting that during my sound meditation workshops, many people report that they enjoy the silence *after* the bell ring completely disappears. This is because the intense awareness of slowly fading sound draws our attention to the arriving silence and rewards us with a new experience – the sound of "silence." People suddenly hear bird calls coming from outside. They hear sounds from far away and they hear sounds from within their bodies. They notice sounds in a new way and ever more intensely than before.

In fact, people say they literally see the physical world in a new luminous way after doing this exercise. Most likely it is because their minds focus on the auditory sense first, and when they finally open their eyes, all of their senses are keener than before, especially their sense of vision. In such a state you are "awakened" and "present" – fully aware of the environment around you and what's inside you.[98]

There are many Zen stories about a guru imparting a *koan* to a student.[99] Here's an example: The master says, "How can the eye see itself without a mirror?" The student is instructed to ponder this riddle for a long time, and the dutiful student considers this question from every possible angle, for months and years on end.

When the student finally has the answer to the *koan*, he or she goes back to the guru and says, "I figured it out! I have the answer to that question you have asked me."

And the guru says, "Yes, so what is the answer?" Regardless of the answer the student offers, the guru may not respond. Instead, the guru might suddenly slap the student or make a sudden loud noise, by shouting, clapping his hands, or vigorously stomping his feet. Then the guru says, "The answer is 'Be here, now!'"

---

98 The significance of using a bell has to do with the "attack" of the bell – its frequency and nature. Because it is vibrating at a high frequency, the sound is bright and clearly noticed by our sense of hearing. In addition, the attack (i.e., the initial moment of sound) is characterized by an immediate rise of the loudness of the sound to the maximum volume of that sound. In other words, the initial volume of a bell is the highest it will be until it fades away and we strike again. We call this behavior a "fast attack." For example, the tambourine and most other percussion instruments have a fast attack.

The bell's high frequency and fast attack cause our mind to pay immediate attention, the way it naturally reacts to alarming sounds (such as a trumpet fanfare or emergency bell). On the contrary, the flute, the clarinet, and the sound of the human voice have a relatively slow attack. These instruments produce a sound that begins with a curvy rise in volume, a rise that is too fast for our consciousness to observe, yet it is a slower rise than the immediate volume climb of the initial sound of a bell or other percussion. Unconsciously, the brain notices the difference between the attack of a bell versus the attack of a flute. That is why alerting sounds use instruments which have a fast attack and vibrate in a high frequency.

99 A *koan* is a paradoxical or knotty problem to meditate upon.

Such is the impact of the sound of the bell: *Be here, now.* That is the deep answer to all the various *koans.* No matter what the question is, that is the universal answer. The slap is just a device to compel the student to leave behind all intellectual thinking and to immediately be fully awake and alert in the present, attuned to the natural environment outside and inside of him. This state of consciousness permits us to be in touch with our intuition, our instincts, and the paradoxical nature of the whole of creation. It is a gateway into a state of being in which we sense the unity and oneness of All that is.

Sound Meditation: Exercise Two

Select some meditative music – preferably performed by a single instrument – such as the oud solo on my CD *Oud Prayers on the Road to St. Jacques.*[100] Turn on the music and then close your eyes. Listen. You may experience an emotional journey, mixed in with some linear, logical thoughts. That is normal. Whatever comes to you is fine, whether thoughts, images, or emotions. Just look at them, acknowledge them, and then move your attention back to the sound of the music.

Try to stick to the sound of the instrument, as if it were a rope. Hold on to it, but not too intensely or obsessively. Hold to it lightly. Cling to the sound without pressure or too much effort. Just ride with it and observe what you hear. Let the sound invade your mind. Enjoy this listening meditation for about ten minutes or until the end of the disk.

Then stop the music when there is a pause in the musical track or during the silence in-between tracks. Hold your attention on the silence as long as you can. This period of silence at the

---

100 You can hear songs on my CD at: www.cdbaby.com/cd/yuval8. Other good selections would be the cello solo in J.S. Bach's *Six Cello Suites*, or the piano solo in J.S. Bach's *Two-Part Inventions*.

end of the music is the most beautiful note! The whole musical journey – the entire rope, that rope of sound you held onto – ultimately leads to this graceful moment of silence. Hopefully, you will experience a taste of bliss in that silence: a stillness, a peacefulness, an emptiness, or a sense of floating. This pleasurable state of awareness is another gateway to accessing the unity of all things, the oneness of All.

When you are done with this exercise, ask yourself: *Was there any pain or tension in my body or any unpleasant mental state that was relieved during the meditation or shortly after it?*

Remember, sound is a set of vibrations that works on your body. It is like receiving a subtle and sophisticated body massage. If sound vibrates the body at an effective frequency and appropriate volume intensity, it yields healing effects. For example, recent studies on the therapeutic use of music have shown that sound enhances treatments for anxiety, depression, and insomnia.[101] Sound also promotes healing following medical procedures.[102]

I have experimented with sound meditation with numerous groups of people around the world, and I have observed how their senses are refreshed and become more sensitive during and after meditation. It is wonderful to witness the transformation

---

101 See "A Neuroscientific Perspective on Music Therapy," by Prof. Koelsch of the University of Sussex, Brighton, UK, indicating that music reduces heart rate, respiratory rate, and blood pressure. See also "The Effects of Music on the Cardiovascular System and Cardiovascular Health," by Prof. Trappe of the University of Bochum, Herne, Germany, which reports that relaxing music significantly decreases the level of anxiety of patients.

102 See "Sound Meditation in Oncological Rehabilitation," by Prof. Jens-Peter Rose of the Klinik fur Tumorbiologie in Freiburg, Germany, which reports that patients who used sound meditation after medical procedures felt more balanced, less nervous, and less exhausted. Also, 75.6% of the patients reported positive body sensations. This research shows that sound meditation is an effective relaxation therapy, which in contrast to some other relaxation methods, does not require regular exercise or practice to achieve positive effects.

that music elicits – the beauty of becoming awakened and attuned, seeing life, relationships, family, friends and nature in a new luminous and optimistic way.

Sound meditation is particularly effective for people who have a hard time meditating any other way. It provides a doorway into the general world of meditative practice. If you can meditate without music, sound meditations may intensify or vary your meditation practice. But, if you have difficulty keeping your mind still, music may be the best tool for quieting and focusing your mind. Yet, please be mindful not to get addicted to the use of music for meditation. In other words, music must not become a crutch you can't do without. Once you establish a routine of meditating with music, gradually reduce the use of music and experiment with meditating to the sound of silence. Also, for experienced meditators the reverse approach works nicely: meditate in silence (108 mindful breaths, for instance) and *then* listen to music.

Sound Meditation: Exercise Three

This is an advanced exercise. You should do this meditation in a space that *allows* audible interruptions and disruptions. Open the windows and let the noisy street sounds come in. Turn on the TV and let a news channel play in the background. Or meditate outdoors in a busy park. The point of this exercise is that life is rarely peaceful. Life is full of distractions that make it difficult to meditate. This is an opportunity to expand yourself and practice peace in a challenging setting.

Listen again to the same meditative music you choose for Exercise Two (the solo instrument selection). Try to hold onto it, despite the interruptions. As you hear the beautiful music, try to calmly flow with the musical line, the progression of notes.

When you hear a noisy interruption, try to visualize yourself expanding *your skin* over that noise. Imagine that *everything* you hear – both the distractions and the music – resides inside your body. Feel your body expand over all the sounds, until the disruptive sounds no longer bother you, just as you are not disturbed by the natural sounds of your own body. Our organs make a variety of noises and in random rhythms. The heart, the stomach, the digestive system are all noisy, but they don't usually bother us. We live in harmony with our internal sounds because they are part of the oneness of our body.

So let's commence this exercise in earnest. Go ahead, replay the deep meditative music and begin meditating on it. And when you hear a disruptive sound, make peace with it and embrace it. Envelop all such noises into your body.

Do this for about ten minutes.

When you are done, sit in silence for as long as you want. Then ask yourself about what happened:

• Have you ever dealt with disruptions as well as you did this time?

• Did the concept of expanding your skin over the interruptions work for you?

• If not, try again.

This exercise, as the others before, should be repeated numerous times with various interrupting sounds. It is a lifelong exploration. This work is about being at peace with everything, every sound, and every living thing.

I experienced this exercise for the first time in 1989 in Boston with a Zen Buddhist master musician who was co-teaching a sound meditation workshop with me at the Boston Center for the Arts. The master had us meditate in silence in between each of the musical tasks. There was a construction site right next to where we were trying to clear and still our minds. The construction noise was extremely loud, and it provided us with a great challenge. Using visualization, most of the people managed to expand themselves to include the disruption within their bodies, and consequently, they made peace with the noise. That was a great testament to the power of the mind and the path of the peaceful warrior.

Many years later, I received a very nice email from one of the participants in a sound meditation workshop which I taught at a retreat center in upstate New York. She wrote that while flying home after the retreat ended, she had an experience that related to the work we did in sound meditation. While having lunch on the airplane, she heard a couple behind her speaking in loud, harsh voices. She simply couldn't stand their argumentative conversation. They were bickering and sniping at each other, on and on, as she was trying to eat mindfully and enjoy her lunch. Their voices were driving her mad! Suddenly, she remembered the exercise she did in my workshop and she thought: *Maybe I can do it right here on the plane.*

So she strived to expand her consciousness over the harsh voices behind her, and she managed to do it. Then she ate her lunch peacefully. She achieved a level of peace despite the disturbance around her. She experienced the transformation, the mental shift that took her from frustration to peace.

You, too, can achieve this type of transformation through sound meditation. May it bring more peace to you and to the world.

APPENDIX B

Meditation Practices
Three Exercises

Meditative and contemplative practices have been part of Judaism, Christianity, Islam, the Asian traditions and every spiritual path I have ever studied. Such practices enrich, nurture, and transform our lives. Below are three meditations drawn from some of the traditions mentioned above.

It is important to dedicate a regular comfortable space in your home for meditation and to do it where distractions are rare, since in most cases a quiet space will help you achieve a deeper and more accessible meditative state. Therefore, establishing a private area for daily meditation aids in developing a healthy routine for your mind. This, in turn, helps you associate that special place with quiet and peace. The result is that your path to cultivating a still and powerful mind will be shorter and more pleasant.

Meditating in the morning sets a positive tone for the rest of the day, but any time is a good time to meditate, unless you are too tired or sleepy. At the start of each meditation, be sure to turn off your cell phone and all electronic devices around you. Sit comfortably, maybe on a pillow on the floor or on a chair. You may close your eyes or leave them open in a narrow blurry gaze. In either case, please remember to start your meditation exercises with slowing down your breath.

The Witness Mind: Exercise One

This meditation is drawn from the Buddhist tradition. Start by sitting still for ten to twenty minutes, focusing on your breath and watching the stream of thoughts that come through your mind. Just witness them, as if they are *not* yours. Try to be like a mirror, which reflects all images without producing any emotions, without getting impressions, and without holding on permanently to any image. Just let these transient thoughts and imaginings flow through you and only temporarily reside in your mind. Simply acknowledge them without getting emotional or judgmental.

After all, these are mere creations of the mind. Just imagine that you are a scientist doing an experiment, observing the mind of *someone else*, impartially watching data pass through. And if a thought or image persists, simply tell it: *I will get back to you later.*

Then imagine yourself breathing out these images. While exhaling, imagine the thought or image flying out of you with the wind of your breath. If you do this often enough – daily is best – you will see positive impacts on your life.[103]

Meditation on Light: Exercise Two

This meditation is drawn from Jewish tradition. First, get a candle and light it. Then sit and fix your eyes on the flame of the candle. Watch the flickering flame for a few minutes.

Now ask the light to come into you. Imagine it streaming into your eyes, your head, your chest, and your heart until it fills your entire body with light.

---

103 See a discussion of the positive impacts of meditation on health, creativity and spirituality in Chapter IV, "Meditation, Unity, and Why You Should Tame the Monkey."

If your mind wanders, bring it back to the sight of the flame. Focus your mind again and again on the light, and do this for about ten to fifteen minutes. Then close your eyes and look for the light inside your body. You may see it between your eyes, in your head, within your chest, and inside your heart. If you lose the sight of the inner light, just partially open your eyes and look at the real candle flame again. That will rekindle the image of the light inside of you, and you will be able to close your eyes and continue to see the light inside your body.

This is an incredibly powerful experience which may change your life positively, if you do it often.

Slow Motion Walking: Exercise Three

This meditation also is drawn from the Buddhist tradition. Start by sitting and slowing your breath. Close your eyes. Then imagine yourself standing up in the slowest manner possible. Like in a slow-motion film, see those parts of your body that assist with the process of standing up begin to move in a slow, gradual, yet fluid motion.

Then, go ahead and do it for real. Stand up using very slow movement. Observe how each of your body parts operates while doing this simple task. Take at least one to two minutes to completely arise from a sitting to standing position. And all the while, keep your eyes in a half gaze, a half-opened and half-closed position.

Now, begin to walk very slowly, still mindful of each single movement and each body part that is involved in the task of walking. Move your feet over the floor in a wave-like motion, with first your heels touching the floor, then the middle of each foot, then the ball of each foot, and lastly your toes. Focus your mind again and again on this snail-paced walk, being mindful of each joint, each bone, and each toe that is involved in the process of walking.

Enjoy this walk for ten to twenty minutes. It may become exhausting. Yet, this slow movement may be so pleasurable, it could become addictive! Hence, the magic of Eastern contemplative movement practices like Tai Chi.

List of Illustrations

Chapter V:	"Meeting of Jalal al-Din Rumi and Molla Shams al-Din"; unknown artist (*circa* 1700)
Chapter VI:	"Rabbi" © Genrikh Bukhsbaum (2001); www.JewishExhibit.com
Chapter VII:	"Pen and Ink Ear Drawing" © Igor Luckyanov (2014); www.Igor-Lukyanov.blogspot.com
Chapter VIII:	"Waves of Resonance" © Gerardo Segismundo (2009); www.SegismundoArt.com

"Yuval at Retreat" © Arielle Kasha (2012) |
Chapter IX:	"Spiritual Portrait of Mevlana Rumi" © Michael Z (2008); published with permission from Technology of the Heart; www.TechofHeart.co
Chapter X:	"St. Hildegard of Bingen," Christian mystic and composer; unknown artist; Eibingen Abbey window, Germany (1753)
Chapter XI:	"Angel with Lute" © Maurice L. Sapiro (1997); www.MauriceSapiro.com
Chapter XII:	"Saxophonist" © Rene Drouyer (2008); www.ReneDrouyer.com

"Yuval with Muse" © Yuval Ron Music (2014); photo by Jorge Vismara |
| **Chapter XIII:** | "Siguiryias" © Marvin Steel (2008); www.MarvinSteel.com |
| **Chapter XIV:** | "The Bowker Meadow"; Dante Gabriel Rossetti (1872) |

Under the Olive Tree

بسم الله الرحمن الرحيم مصر يج بجلوب نعت شجرة الزيتون

Sacred Music of the Middle East

The Yuval Ron Ensemble

featuring Najwa Gibran

Seeker of Truth

The Yuval Ron Ensemble

Live at the World Festival of Sacred Music

Featuring vocalist
Najwa Gibran

With special guest Qawwali master
Sukhawat Ali Khan

About the Author

Yuval Ron is a world-renowned musician, composer, educator, peace activist, and record producer. He is the creative force behind the multi-faith Yuval Ron Ensemble, which regularly conducts "Peace Tours" throughout the Middle East and around the world.

Among his many achievements, Yuval composed the music for the Oscar winning film *West Bank Story*. In 2008, he was honored to perform for the Dalai Lama at the Seeds of Compassion Festival. In addition, Yuval has collaborated with Sufi leader Pir Zia Inayat-Khan, master musician Omar Faruk Tekbilek, Zen Buddhist priest and visual artist Hirokazu Kosaka, choreographers Daniel Ezralow and Oguri, and leading neuroscientists Mark Robert Waldman and Andrew Newberg, M.D.

In 2004, Yuval received the Los Angeles Treasures Award. He also is the recipient of grants from the National Endowment for the Arts, American Composers Forum, California Council for the Humanities, and the Rockefeller Foundation.

Yuval is a noted lecturer and has been invited to speak at numerous universities, including Yale, Johns Hopkins, UCLA, MIT, Berklee College of Music, University of Chicago, and many others. Yuval has been on the faculty of Esalen Institute since 2009, and he is an affiliated artist with the Center for Jewish Culture and Creativity and a "Guiding Voice" for Seven Pillars House of Wisdom.

To hear Yuval's music, see his concert schedule, and learn more about his recordings, books, master-classes, and workshops, please visit his website.

www.YuvalRonMusic.com

The Oracle Institute Press, LLC

A division of The Oracle Institute
A 501(c)(3) educational charity
1990 Battlefield Drive
Independence, Virginia 24348

An Advocate for Peace and
A Vanguard for Conscious Evolution

All donations and proceeds from our books and classes are used to further our educational mission and to build the Peace Pentagon, an interfaith and social justice center in Independence, Virginia.

www.TheOracleInstitute.org

About the Publisher

The Truth

The Oracle Institute chose the Pentacle as its icon to represent spiritual unity among the five primary religions: *Hinduism, Judaism, Buddhism, Christianity, and Islam.* These religions – like nearly all of the political, economic, and social systems crafted by mankind – are based on patriarchy and hierarchy. Oracle believes the time has come for humanity to shed archaic belief systems about the Godhead and prepare for the next phase of our collective Conscious Evolution.

The Love

Oracle promotes the *Saddha* process of soul growth, which includes study, worship, meditation, and the performance of good works through application of the Golden Rule – the "Eleventh Commandment" in the Christian tradition brought to us by Jesus. When we earnestly strive to perfect ourselves, practice compassion toward others, and assume responsibility for the health of humanity and our planet, we help birth the new Spiritual Paradigm.

The Light

In the Holy Books and Wisdom Teachings of all traditions, there are prophecies about recreating "Heaven on Earth." To manifest this new era of harmony and abundance – what Oracle calls the "Fifth Spiritual Paradigm" – humanity must first rebalance the Godhead with Sacred Feminine energy. To that end, Oracle offers interfaith books, spirituality classes, peace-building programs, and holistic products designed to foster the quest for Spiritual Enlightenment and Planetary Peace.

CPSIA information can be obtained at www.ICGtesting.com
Printed in the USA
LVOW08s0705030814

397248LV00001B/116/P

9 781937 465162